Contents

To WLIW

LEADING

IN A CULTURE OF

CHANGE

Published by Jossey-Bass
A Wiley Imprint
989 Market Street, San Francisco, CA 94103-1741   www.josseybass.com

Copyright page continued on p. 166.

Limit of Liability/Disclaimer of Warranty: While the publisher and author have used their best efforts in preparing this book, they make no representations or warranties with respect to the accuracy or completeness of the contents of this book and specifically disclaim any implied warranties of merchantability or fitness for a particular purpose. No warranty may be created or extended by sales representatives or written sales materials. The advice and strategies contained herein may not be suitable for your situation. You should consult with a professional where appropriate. Neither the publisher nor author shall be liable for any loss of profit or any other commercial damages, including but not limited to special, incidental, consequential, or other damages.

Readers should be aware that Internet Web sites offered as citations and/or sources for further information may have changed or disappeared between the time this was written and when it is read.

Jossey-Bass books and products are available through most bookstores. To contact Jossey-Bass directly call our Customer Care Department within the U.S. at 800-956-7739, outside the U.S. at 317-572-3986, or fax 317-572-4002.

Jossey-Bass also publishes its books in a variety of electronic formats. Some content that appears in print may not be available in electronic books.

Library of Congress Cataloging-in-Publication Data
Fullan, Michael.
   Leading in a culture of change : being effective in complex times / Michael Fullan.
      p. cm.
Includes bibliographical references (p.   ) and index.
   ISBN-13 978-0-7879-5395-9 (alk. paper)
   ISBN-10 0-7879-5395-4 (alk. paper)
   ISBN-13 978-0-7879-8766-4 (paperback)
   ISBN-10 0-7879-8766-2 (paperback)
   1. Educational leadership.   2. School management and organization.
3. Educational change.   I. Title.
   LB2806 .F794 2001
   371.2—dc21   2001002014

Printed in the United States of America
FIRST EDITION
HB Printing   20 19 18 17 16 15 14 13 12 1
PB Printing   10 9 8 7 6 5

Preface

THE MORE COMPLEX SOCIETY GETS, THE MORE SOPHIS-
ticated leadership must become. Complexity means
change, but specifically it means rapidly occurring, unpredictable, nonlinear change. Moreover, the pace of change is
ever increasing, as James Gleick, the author of *Chaos*, point-
ed out in a recent book called *Faster*, which he subtitled *The
Acceleration of Just About Everything* (Gleick, 1999). How
do you lead in a culture such as ours, which seems to spe-
cialize in pell-mell innovation?

This is the leader's dilemma. On the one hand, failing to
act when the environment around you is radically changing
leads to extinction. On the other hand, making quick decisions under conditions of mind-racing mania can be equally
fatal. Robert Steinberg said it best: "The essence of intelligence would seem to be in knowing when to think and act

quickly, and knowing when to think and act slowly" (cited in Gleick, 1999, p. 114).

This book is about how leaders can focus on certain key change themes that will allow them to lead effectively under messy conditions. The book is also about how leaders foster leadership in others, thereby making themselves dispensable in the long run. And it is about how we can produce more "leaders of leaders."

The good news is that society has not been evolving as recklessly as it seems. As we shall see, there are deep theoretical reasons why change occurs as it does. If we can come to understand these powerful themes, we will be able to influence (but not control) them for the better. I identify these themes in Chapter One, which I call "A Remarkable Convergence" because certain powerful factors have emerged that have developed independently but that are deeply compatible—indeed, synergistic. There are five themes in particular: moral purpose, understanding change, developing relationships, knowledge building, and coherence making. Chapters Two through Six take each theme in turn and examine in more detail its inner workings. Through these five chapters I develop a comprehensive theory of leadership. In Chapter Seven, I take up the matter of becoming a leader and how systems can foster leadership development, which turns out to be more of a tortoise than a hare proposition. Leadership must be cultivated deliberately over time at all levels of the organization.

Two things have happened in recent times that aid our pursuit of effective leadership. One is that the knowledge base for what makes for success under conditions of complexity is getting better—deeper, more insightful. The other is that there are many more case examples of large-scale transformation in both business and education. There is literally more to learn today than ever before. Since the early 1990s we have begun to study and learn from more and more examples of purposeful reform. We are uncovering fantastic new insights from these experiences. This book draws from these new ideas in both business and education, and in so doing finds remarkable convergences in what we are discovering about how to lead in a culture of complex change.

Leadership in business and in education increasingly have more in common. As we shall see, businesses are realizing more and more that having moral purpose is critical for sustainable success. In this respect they have much to learn from schools. Schools are beginning to discover that new ideas, knowledge creation, and sharing are essential to solving learning problems in a rapidly changing society. Schools can learn from how the best companies innovate and get results. At the most basic level, businesses and schools are similar in that in the knowledge society, they both must become *learning organizations* or they will fail to survive. Thus, leaders in business and education face similar challenges—how to cultivate and sustain learning under conditions of complex, rapid change.

Fortunately, there are many more examples of organizations that are engaged in successful change. I have benefited from working with a growing number of colleagues in Toronto and around the world helping bring about (and study) large-scale reform. The most interesting initiative is our critical friend evaluation of the National Literacy and Numeracy Strategy in England, in which dramatic improvements in student performance are being attempted in all the primary schools in the country (twenty thousand) over a five-year period (1997 to 2002); actually, more schools will be involved, because the results must extend beyond the primary schools into secondary schools and into the infrastructure. I thank my colleagues Lorna Earl, Ken Leithwood, Ben Levin, Nancy Watson, Doris Jantzi, Blair Mascall, and Nancy Torrance for their work on the England evaluation.

We are also working on several other fronts: school district reform, such as the literacy project involving ninety-three schools in the Toronto District School Board; the study of literacy reform in the York Region District School Board; the development of "assessment literacy" in all eighty-four schools (and thus in the system) in the Edmonton Catholic School District; the Manitoba School Improvement Program; and the evaluation of school improvement in the Guilford County School District in Greensboro, North Carolina. We are also trying our hand at the redesign of teacher education, both in Toronto in our own program and in Louisiana, where comprehensive reform of teacher education and school improvement is being attempted. At the same time, we have monitored large-scale change projects conducted by others around the world. Andy Hargreaves and Carol Rolheiser have been particularly helpful in working through many of the ideas as we drew lessons from educational reform initiatives.

Clearly these are exciting times—there is a lot going on. Not the least of these developments is the new realization that leadership is key to large-scale improvement yet must be radically different than it has been. Further, effective leadership is in very short supply. We can therefore expect to see leadership development initiatives dominating the scene over the next decade.

Leadership required in a culture of change, however, is not straightforward. We are living in chaotic conditions. Thus leaders must be able to operate under complex, uncertain circumstances. For this reason, I dedicate this book to a chaos theory concept, "wildness lies in wait." Bernstein (1996, p. 331) quotes G. K. Chesterton: "The real trouble with this world of ours is not that it is an unreasonable world, or even that it is a reasonable one. The commonest kind of trouble is that it is nearly reasonable, but not quite. Life is not an illogicality; yet it is a trap for logicians. It looks just a little more mathematical and regular than it is; its exactitude is obvious, but its inexactitude is hidden; its wildness lies in wait."

Not a bad mantra for leaders in complex times: seek out and honor hidden inexactitudes.

April 2001   Michael Fullan
Toronto, Ontario, Canada

Chapter One

A Remarkable Convergence

CHANGE IS A DOUBLE-EDGED SWORD. ITS RELENTLESS pace these days runs us off our feet. Yet when things are unsettled, we can find new ways to move ahead and to create breakthroughs not possible in stagnant societies. If you ask people to brainstorm words to describe change, they come up with a mixture of negative and positive terms. On the one side, *fear, anxiety, loss, danger, panic;* on the other, *exhilaration, risk-taking, excitement, improvements, energizing.* For better or for worse, change arouses emotions, and when emotions intensify, leadership is key.

This is not a book about superleaders. Charismatic leaders inadvertently often do more harm than good because, at best, they provide episodic improvement followed by frustrated or despondent dependency. Superhuman leaders also do us another disservice: they are role models who can never be emulated by large numbers. Deep and sustained reform depends on many of us, not just on the very few who are destined to be extraordinary.

This book, then, is about how all of us can improve our leadership by focusing on a small number of key dimensions. Each and every leader, whether the CEO of a multinational corporation or a school principal, can become more effective—much more effective—by focusing on a small number of core aspects of leadership and by developing a new mind-set about the leader's responsibility to himself or herself and to those with whom he or she works.

I have never been fond of distinguishing between leadership and management: they overlap and you need both qualities. But here is one difference that it makes sense to highlight: leadership is needed for problems that do not have easy answers. The big problems of the day are complex, rife with paradoxes and dilemmas. For these problems there are no once-and-for-all answers. Yet we expect our leaders to provide solutions. We place leaders in untenable positions (or, alternatively, our system produces leaders who try to carry the day with populist, one-sided solutions that are as clear as they are oversimplified). Homer-Dixon (2000b, p. 15) makes a similar observation: "We demand that [leaders] solve, or at least manage, a multitude of interconnected problems that can develop into crises without warning; we require them to navigate an increasingly turbulent reality that is, in key aspects, literally incomprehensible to the human mind; we buffet them on every side with bolder, more powerful special interests that challenge every innovative policy idea; we submerge them in often unhelpful and distracting information; and we force them to decide and act at an ever faster pace."

Heifetz (1994) accuses us of looking for the wrong kind of leadership when the going gets tough: "in a crisis . . . we call for someone with answers, decision, strength, and a map of the future, someone who knows where we ought to be going—in short someone who can make hard problems simple. . . . Instead of looking for saviors, we should be calling for leadership that will challenge us to face problems for which there are no simple, painless solutions—problems that require us to learn new ways" (p. 21).

An alternative image of leadership, argues Heifetz (1994, p. 15), is one of "mobilizing people to tackle tough problems." Leadership, then, is not mobilizing others to solve problems we already know how to solve, but to help them confront problems that have never yet been successfully addressed.

There is, I will argue, a recent remarkable convergence of theories, knowledge bases, ideas, and strategies that help us confront complex problems that do not have easy answers. This convergence creates a new mind-set—a framework for thinking about and leading complex change more powerfully than ever before. Figure 1.1 summarizes the framework.

There are strong reasons to believe that five components of leadership represent independent but mutual reinforcing forces for positive change. Chapters Two through Six are devoted to building the case for the powerful knowledge base represented by these five components of effective leadership. In the following paragraphs I will discuss Figure 1.1, providing a brief overview of the components.

Briefly, *moral purpose* means acting with the intention of making a positive difference in the lives of employees, customers, and society as a whole. This is an obvious value with

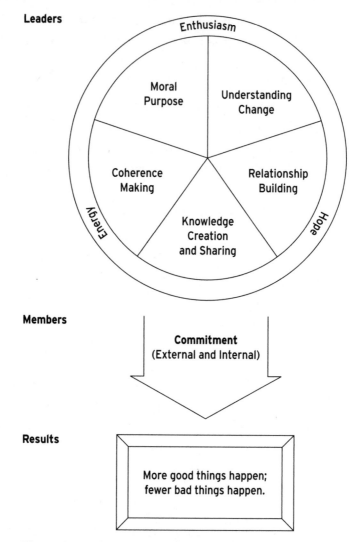

Figure 1.1. A Framework for Leadership.

which many of us can identify, but I will argue in Chapter Two that there may be inevitable evolutionary reasons why moral purpose will become more and more prominent and that, in any case, to be effective in complex times, leaders must be guided by moral purpose. In Chapter Two we will take up case studies from both business and education that will demonstrate that moral purpose is critical to the long-term success of all organizations.

Second, it is essential for leaders to *understand the change process*. Moral purpose without an understanding of change will lead to moral martyrdom. Moreover, leaders who combine a commitment to moral purpose with a healthy respect for the complexities of the change process not only will be more successful but also will unearth deeper moral purpose. Understanding the change process is exceedingly elusive. Management books contain reams of advice, but the advice is often contradictory, general, and at the end of the day confusing and nonactionable. Chapter Three identifies these problems and offers six guidelines that provide leaders with concrete and novel ways of thinking about the process of change: (1) the goal is not to innovate the most; (2) it is not enough to have the best ideas; (3) appreciate early difficulties of trying something new—what I call the implementation dip; (4) redefine resistance as a potential positive force; (5) reculturing is the name of the game; (6) never a checklist, always complexity.

Third, we have found that the single factor common to every successful change initiative is that *relationships* improve. If relationships improve, things get better. If they remain the same or get worse, ground is lost. Thus leaders must be consummate relationship builders with diverse people and groups—especially with people different than themselves. Effective leaders constantly foster purposeful interaction and problem solving, and are wary of easy consensus.

Fourth, the new work on *knowledge creation and sharing*

reflects an amazing congruence with the previous three themes. We live, after all, in the knowledge society, but that term is a cliché. What is deeply revealing is that new theoretical and empirical studies of successful organizations unpack the operational meaning of the general term "knowledge organization." I will show how leaders commit themselves to constantly generating and increasing knowledge inside and outside the organization. What is astonishing (because it comes from an independent theoretical tradition) is how intimately the role of knowledge relates to the previous three themes. What has been discovered is that, first, people will not voluntarily share knowledge unless they feel some moral commitment to do so; second, people will not share unless the dynamics of change favor exchange; and, third, that data without relationships merely cause more information glut. Put another way, turning information into knowledge is a *social* process, and for that you need good relationships. So Chapter Five focuses on knowledge building, but we will see that we need moral purpose, an understanding of the change process, and good relationships if we are to create and share knowledge.

All this complexity keeps people on the edge of chaos. It is important to be on that edge because that is where creativity resides, but anarchy lurks there too. Therefore, effective leaders tolerate enough ambiguity to keep the creative juices flowing, but along the way (once they and the group know enough), they seek coherence. *Coherence making* is a perennial pursuit. Leadership is difficult in a culture of change because disequilibrium is common (and valuable, provided that patterns of coherence can be fostered).

In summary, moral purpose is concerned with direction

and results; understanding change, building relationships, and knowledge building honor the complexity and discovery of the journey; and coherence making extracts valuable patterns worth retaining. But, alas, none of this is quite so linear and fixed as it would seem when one reads a simple description of each component.

There is another set of seemingly more personal characteristics that all effective leaders possess, which I have labeled the *energy-enthusiasm-hopefulness* constellation. I do not think it is worth debating whether this constellation is a cause or an effect of the five leadership components. No doubt there is a dynamic, reciprocal relationship between the two sets. Energetic-enthusiastic-hopeful leaders "cause" greater moral purpose in themselves, bury themselves in change, naturally build relationships and knowledge, and seek coherence to consolidate moral purpose. Looking at the dynamic from the "other side," we can see that leaders immersed in the five aspects of leadership can't help feeling and acting more energetic, enthusiastic, and hopeful. Whatever the case, effective leaders make people feel that even the most difficult problems can be tackled productively. They are always hopeful—conveying a sense of optimism and an attitude of never giving up in the pursuit of highly valued goals. Their enthusiasm and confidence (not certainty) are, in a word, infectious, and they are infectiously effective, provided that they incorporate all five leadership capacities in their day-to-day behavior.

Note also how the five capacities together operate in a checks and balances fashion. Leaders with deep moral purpose provide guidance, but they can also have blinders if ideas are not challenged through the dynamics of change, the give and take of relationships, and the ideas generated by new knowledge. Similarly, coherence is seen as part and parcel of complexity and can never be completely achieved. Leaders in a culture of change value and almost enjoy the tensions inherent in addressing hard-to-solve problems, because that is where the greatest accomplishments lie.

Figure 1.1 also shows how leaders who are steeped in the five core capacities by definition evince and generate long-term commitment in those with whom they work. Effective leaders, because they live and breathe the five aspects of leadership, find themselves committed to stay the course (in a sense, they are also inspired by others in the organization as they interact around moral purposes, new knowledge, and the achievement of periodic coherence), and, of course, they mobilize more and more people to become willing to tackle tough problems. We have to be careful when we talk about commitment. In the past, we have written about blind commitment or groupthink—when the group goes along uncritically with the leader or the group (Fullan & Hargreaves, 1992). Leaders can be powerful, and so can groups, which means they can be powerfully wrong. This is why the five dimensions of leadership must work in concert. They provide a check against uninformed commitment.

Even when commitment is evidently generated, there are qualifiers. Argyris (2000, p. 40) has helped us make the crucial distinction between *external* and *internal* commitment: "These differ in how they are activated and in the source of energy they utilize. External commitment is triggered by management policies and practices that enable employees to accomplish their tasks. Internal commitment derives from energies internal to human beings that are activated because getting a job done is intrinsically rewarding." Argyris notes that "when someone else defines objectives, goals, and the steps to be taken to reach them, whatever commitment exists will be external" (p. 41).

Moral purpose is usually accompanied by a sense of urgency. Leaders in some such cases are in a hurry. If they are in too much of a hurry, they will completely fail—you can't bulldoze change. If leaders are more sophisticated, they may set up a system of pressure and support, which in the short run will obtain noticeable desired results, but these will mainly be derived from external commitment. Remember that external commitment is still commitment; it is the motivation to put one's effort into the task of change. It can include excitement and satisfaction of accomplishment. It is valuable. Later, I will present case studies of change projects that generated a good deal of external commitment with impressive short-term results. But we will also discuss the ins and outs of developing internal commitment on a large scale—an extremely difficult proposition.

At this stage of the discussion, we need only make the point essential to the framework illustrated in Figure 1.1. The litmus test of all leadership is whether it mobilizes people's commitment to putting their energy into actions designed to improve things. It is individual commitment, but it is above all collective mobilization. We will also see in subsequent chapters that collective action by itself can be short-lived if it is not based on or does not lead to a deep sense of internal purpose among organizational members. Generating internal over external commitment and external over blind commitment is the mark of effective leadership.

What are the outcomes of all this effective leadership and commitment? In Figure 1.1, I have deliberately referred to results very generally as causing "more good things to happen" and "fewer bad things to happen." I will be presenting case studies from both business and education. In the case of business, good things are economic viability, customer satisfaction, employee pride, and a sense of being valuable to society. In schools, good things are enhanced student performance, increased capacity of teachers, greater involvement of parents and community members, engagement of students, all-around satisfaction and enthusiasm about going further, and greater pride for all in the system. In both cases, the reduction of bad things means fewer aborted change efforts; less demoralization of employees; fewer examples of piecemeal, uncoordinated reform; and a lot less wasted effort and resources.

This book delves into the complexities of leadership evidenced in Figure 1.1. It provides insights, strategies, and, ultimately, better theories of knowledge and action suited to leadership in complex times. In the final chapter we will examine more directly the question of how new leaders can be developed. How to become more effective as a leader is of growing concern for all those in positions to make a difference; how to foster large numbers of leaders in all areas of society is a system question more worrisome today than ever before. If leadership does not become more attractive, doable, and exciting, public and private institutions will deteriorate. If the experience of rank-and-file members of the organization does not improve, there will not be a pool of potential leaders to cultivate. A classic chicken-and-egg problem. Good leaders foster good leadership at other levels. Leadership at other levels produces a steady stream of future leaders for the system as a whole.

The conclusion, then, is that leaders will increase their effectiveness if they continually work on the five components of leadership—if they pursue moral purpose, understand the change process, develop relationships, foster knowledge building, and strive for coherence—with energy, enthusiasm, and hopefulness. If leaders do so, the rewards and benefits will be enormous. It is an exciting proposition. The culture of change beckons.

Chapter Two

Moral Purpose

YOU DON'T HAVE TO BE MOTHER THERESA TO HAVE
moral purpose. Some people are deeply passionate
about improving life (sometimes to a fault, if they lack one or
more of the other four components of leadership: understanding of the change process, strong relationships, knowledge
building, and coherence making among multiple priorities).
Others have a more cognitive approach, displaying less emo-
tion but still being intensely committed to betterment.
Whatever one's style, every leader, to be effective, must have
and work on improving his or her moral purpose.

Moral purpose is about both ends and means. In education, an important end is to make a difference in the lives of
students. But the means of getting to that end are also crucial.
If you don't treat others (for example, teachers) well and
fairly, you will be a leader without followers (see Chapter

Four, in which I describe how effective leaders constantly work on developing relationships at all levels of the organization). Of course, a case can be made that leading with integrity is not just instrumental. To strive to improve the quality of how we live together is a moral purpose of the highest order. Sergiovanni (1999, p. 17) draws the same conclusion about what he calls the lifeworld of leadership.

> Ask the next five people you meet to list three persons they know, either personally or from history, who they consider to be authentic leaders. Then have them describe these leaders. Chances are your respondents will mention integrity, reliability, moral excellence, a sense of purpose, firmness of conviction, steadiness, and unique qualities of style and substance that differentiate the leaders they choose from others. Key in this list of characteristics is the importance of substance, distinctive qualities, and moral underpinnings. Authentic leaders anchor their practice in ideas, values, and commitments, exhibit distinctive qualities of style and substance, and can be trusted to be morally diligent in advancing the enterprises they lead. Authentic leaders, in other words, display character, and character is the defining characteristic of authentic leadership.

At the loftiest level, moral purpose is about how humans evolve over time, especially in relation to how they relate to each other. Ridley (1996) and Sober and Wilson (1998) trace the evolution of self-centered and cooperative behavior in animals, insects, and humans. What makes humans different, says Ridley, is culture. Ideas, knowledge, practices and beliefs, and the like enter consciousness and can be passed on "by direct infection from one person to another" (p. 179). Ridley raises the interesting evolutionary hypothesis that "cooperative groups thrive and selfish ones do not, so cooperative societies have survived at the expense of others" (p. 175). Thus leaders in all organizations, whether they know it or not, contribute for better or for worse to moral purpose in their own organizations and in society as a whole.

Sober and Wilson (1998) also state that it is futile to argue whether people are driven by egoistic (self-centered) or altruistic (unselfish) motives. The fact is that all effective leaders are driven by both—what Sober and Wilson call "motivational pluralism[, which] is the view that we have both egoistic and altruistic ultimate desires" (p. 308). This is why everyday leaders shouldn't expect to be like Mother Theresa. (And who knows, maybe she got a lot of pleasure out of helping others). Most of us have mixed motives, and that is perfectly fine.

I will also show that moral purpose doesn't stand alone. We will see that leaders who work on the five qualities in this book—not just the obvious first quality, which is moral purpose itself, but all four other components—will, by definition, find themselves steeped in moral purpose. Whether you are an insurance executive or a school principal, you simply cannot be effective without behaving in a morally purposeful way. And if you follow the lessons in this book, you won't have to *plan* to be more moral in your pursuit; it will come naturally. Moral purpose is profoundly built into the five components of leadership as they are carried out in practice.

The complexity of pursuing moral purpose in a culture of change can be best illustrated through case examples. I select cases equally from education and from business to show that the issues of leadership are increasingly common across both types of organizations. A major education example comes from our current multiyear large-scale evaluation of the National Literacy and Numeracy Strategy in England.

The Case of the National Literacy and Numeracy Strategy

Let us descend from this elevated abstract level and consider a real case, a very large scale case involving a whole country (twenty thousand schools with seven million students up to age eleven), namely the case of the National Literacy and Numeracy Strategy (NLNS) in England. Here is the proposition: a new government comes into power in 1997, and the prime minister declares that his three priorities are "education, education, education." We have heard that before, but this government goes further. It says that the initial core goal is to raise the literacy and numeracy achievement of children up to age eleven. The government sets specific targets. The baseline they observe is that the percentage of eleven-year-olds scoring 4 or 5 on the test of literacy was 57 percent in 1996 (level 4 being the level at which proficiency standards are met); for numeracy the baseline was 54 percent. The minister announces that the targets for 2002 are 80 percent for literacy (up from 57 percent) and 75 percent for numeracy (up from 54 percent). He makes a commitment that he will resign as secretary of state if those targets are not met.

Further, the leaders of the initiative in the Department for Education and Employment set out to "use the change knowledge base" to design a set of pressure-and-support strategies to accomplish this remarkable feat. Finally, they know they are going to be watched carefully as this highly political and highly explicit initiative unfolds. A team of us at the University of Toronto are monitoring and assessing the entire NLNS strategy as it unfolds during the 1998 to 2002 period.

The main elements of the implementation strategy are summarized by Michael Barber (2000, pp. 8–9), head of the government initiative:

- A nationally prepared project plan for both literacy and numeracy, setting out actions, responsibilities, and deadlines through to 2002;

- A substantial investment sustained over at least six years and skewed toward those schools that need most help;

- A project infrastructure involving national direction from the Standards and Effectiveness Unit, 15 regional directors, and over 300 expert consultants at the local level for each of the two strategies;

- An expectation that every class will have a daily math lesson and daily literacy hour;

- A detailed teaching programme covering every school year for children from ages 5 to 11;

- An emphasis on early intervention and catch up for pupils who fall behind;

- A professional development programme designed to enable every primary school teacher to learn to understand and use proven best practices in both curriculum areas;

- The appointment of over 2,000 leading math teachers and hundreds of expert literacy teachers who have the time and skill to model best practice for their peers;

- The provision of "intensive support" to circa half of all schools where the most progress is required;

- A major investment in books for schools (over 23 million new books in the system since May 1997);

- The removal of barriers to implementation (especially a huge reduction in prescribed curriculum content outside the core subjects);

- Regular monitoring and extensive evaluation by our national inspection agency, OFSTED;

- A national curriculum for initial teacher training requiring all providers to prepare new primary school teachers to teach the daily math lesson and the literacy hour;

- A problem-solving philosophy involving early identification of difficulties as they emerge and the provision of rapid solutions or intervention where necessary;

- The provision of extra after-school, weekend, and holiday booster classes for those who need extra help to reach the standard.

The impact of the strategies on achievement, measured as a percentage of pupils reaching levels 4 or 5, is in many ways astounding (recall that twenty thousand schools are involved). By the year 2000, the whole country had progressively moved from 57 percent proficient achievement in literacy in 1996 to 75 percent; and from 54 percent to 72 percent in numeracy. We have no doubt that the targets of 80 percent and 75 percent will be achieved by 2002, although I do not present it as a problem-free case because a preoccupation with achievement scores can have negative side effects, such as narrowing the curriculum that is taught and burning people out as they relentlessly chase targets.

There is a lot more than moral purpose operating in this case, and we will draw on it again in subsequent chapters. I use it here to illustrate the value and dilemmas of moral purpose. In terms of moral purpose, there are several points to be made. First, getting thousands of students to be literate and numerate who otherwise would not be so is not a bad day's work. This is bound to make a difference in many lives.

Second, moral purpose cannot just be stated, it must be accompanied by strategies for realizing it, and those strategies are the leadership actions that energize people to pursue a desired goal. In a recent interview in the *Times Education Supplement,* "Charisma and Loud Shouting" (2000, p. 28), Sir Michael Bichard, the permanent secretary at the Department for Education and Employment in England, said it this way: "For me leadership is about creating a sense of purpose and direction. It's about getting alignment and it's about inspiring people to achieve. . . . [There is a] need to enthuse staff and encourage a belief in the difference their organization is making—whether it is a school or a government department. We can do a lot by making heroes of the people who deliver. It's important to make people feel part of a success story. That's what they want to be."

Third, pluralistic motives abound. The government wants to be reelected, *and* leaders may get a lot of personal gratification if it is successful, *and* their careers may be enhanced, *and* there is an explicit measurable purpose.

Fourth, who knows whether this is a right purpose? Is there collateral damage: do other subjects like the arts suffer? Are schools becoming preoccupied only by the test results? Are teachers getting burnt out? Will short-term success be followed by deeper failure? And so on.

Fifth, is the strategy really inspiring people (principals and teachers, for example) to do better? How deep is their commitment? I have written about this case elsewhere (Fullan, 2001), and there are numerous legitimate questions about the National Literacy and National Numeracy Strategy case. Our conclusion at this stage is that the strategy has indeed caught the interest and energy of the majority of principals and teachers and that they are getting a sense of pride and accomplishment from the results so far. Nevertheless, to use Argyris's terms, the leadership strategy has generated only external commitment on the part of school educators—albeit real commitment that got real results. In order to go deeper, for example, to get at the creative ideas and energies of teachers, additional leadership strategies will be needed—strategies that will foster internal commitment (that is, commitment activated by intrinsically rewarding accomplishments).

In summary, leadership, if it is to be effective, has to (1) have an explicit "making-a-difference" sense of purpose, (2) use strategies that mobilize many people to tackle tough problems, (3) be held accountable by measured and debatable indicators of success, and (4) be ultimately assessed by the extent to which it awakens people's intrinsic commitment, which is none other than the mobilizing of everyone's sense of moral purpose.

The Case of Monsanto

Pascale, Millemann, and Gioja (2000) report on the case of Monsanto, a life science company that underwent a remarkable transformation in the years 1993 to 1999 under the direction of its new CEO, Robert Shapiro. Shapiro used a series of "town hall meetings" to introduce the new direction and to begin a dialogue. Pascale et al. (pp. 80–81) quote at length from one of Shapiro's presentations in 1995, attended by three hundred of the company's informal leaders:

> Here's what bothers me. There are almost six billion people in the world but the global economy works for only one billion of them. Even for the favored group (and the two billion that are about to join it), there are rising expectations as to the amounts, choice, quality, and health of food. At the other end of the continuum, at least one and a half billion of the world's population are in real trouble. Eight hundred million of these are so malnourished that they cannot participate in work or family life and are on the edge of starvation. Finally, over the next thirty years, most of the additional people joining the planet will be born in poorer places.
>
> The system we have is unsustainable. We burn a lot of hydrocarbons and waste a lot of stuff. There is not enough acreage on earth to provide for humanity's food needs using traditional technology. In developed countries there is the interesting challenge of aging. The elderly consume a lot of

health care as technology offers more costly interventions. Fewer people in the workforce end up supporting the higher bill for those who are old. This, too, is politically unsustainable.

Food is shifting from an issue of fuel and calories to an issue of choice. With growing nutritional and environmental consciousness, food must inevitably command a larger share of mind.

These problems for humanity can also be seen as a trillion-dollar opportunity. These are all unresolved problems. It isn't just a question of modular extensions of what we have (via technology and innovations in distribution). We need to reinvent our approach fundamentally. Biotechnol-ogy is a profoundly different avenue for agriculture and human health. And information technology provides enough of a difference in degree that it represents a nanotechnology. Biotechnology is really a subset of information technology. It does not deal with the information that's encoded electronically in silicon but with the information that is encoded chemically in cells, not used for E-mail or spreadsheets but information that tells what proteins to make, when to make them, and how to make them. The rate of increase of knowledge in this field puts Moore's Law to shame, doubling every twelve to eighteen months. We will map the entire human genome by 2005, and will understand most of the functionality of the genome in this same period.

I believe our agriculture and health care systems will be revolutionized by the intersection of biotechnology and information technology. There is something of great consequence in the convergence of these technologies with our market knowledge, and I want you to help me discover what it is.

Pascale and his colleagues portray the interplay between Shapiro, as leader, and the employees: "Shapiro points to pieces in the puzzle (life sciences breakthroughs, agriculture, information technology, market knowledge); listeners relate his words to their own experience and fill in the blanks with their detailed knowledge of the business; Shapiro focuses on the *unsustainable* problems facing humanity—immense challenges that cry out for nontraditional solutions" (p. 81). The authors observe: "many in the room are moved at the prospect of contributing to the elimination of world hunger and chronic suffering" (p. 83). All of this sounds very much like moral purpose. Ideas, energy, and action follow, with some ten thousand of Monsanto's thirty thousand employees becoming involved. Through leadership that mobilized the energies and ideas of employees, Monsanto made a rapid impact in the market. The consulting firm McKinsey called it one of the most thoroughgoing transformations in business history (p. 86).

Pascale et al. note: "Within three years following Monsanto's introduction of genetically modified seeds, farms had shifted 50 percent of all cotton and 40 percent of all soybeans grown in the United States to disease- and herbicide-resistant crops. American cotton growers alone reduced herbicide consumption by $1 billion" (p. 6). The share price, they report, "rocketed from $16 to $63" (p. 86).

It would be too simple if we concluded that Monsanto was an out and out success. There was growing objection on environmental grounds to genetically modified seeds; Monsanto initially regarded this objection as political backlash and as a public relations problem. Shapiro and his colleagues still felt that they were making a valuable contribution to the world, but by 1999 Shapiro finally acknowledged: "Our confidence in this technology and our enthusiasm for it has, I think, widely been seen, and understandably so, as condescension or indeed arrogance. Because we thought it was our job to persuade, too often we forget to listen" (Pascale et al., 2000, p. 87).

Today, Monsanto has merged with Upjohn to form Pharmacia, with Shapiro as nonexecutive chairman. It is too early to tell how well Pharmacia will pursue the moral issues embedded in its biotechnology goals. It is still a strong financial competitor, but what are the lessons here? First, a sense of moral purpose on the part of employees is important and can make a huge difference in the performance of the organization. Second, and of growing significance in the global economy, moral purpose applies outside as well as inside the company. Pascale et al. put it this way:

> [H]ow a system connects with its external world is also a key source of that system's health. Connectivity is not just about good relations with those outside the company. It impacts the quality of strategy and design and has direct bearing on a company's success.
>
> Biotechnology presents just one example of issues that are too complex to address without a design for broadening the participation of people with diverse concerns and stakes in the questions. Seeking out the views of scientists and government regulators, people affected in different ways by the product help everyone imagine and design for unintended consequences. To talk only to oneself as a company will lead to strategic vulnerability [Pascale et al., 2000, p. 91].

Commitment to the environment and to the broader global community as part and parcel of the long-term success of the organization is moral purpose writ large. Pascale and his colleagues conclude, "we can no longer afford to look at our business as atomistic agents alone in a world to which we connect only through competition" (2000, p. 92). If you want more than short-term gains, moral purpose sincerely sought is good for business. Pluralistic motives can coexist: do good, worry about the environment, and derive a profit. But leaders have to be explicitly aware of the interplay of these three forces.

I do not for a minute think that moral purpose automatically attracts people to do good things. Acting with moral purpose in a complex world is, as we have just seen, highly problematic. First, there are many, many competing "goods," which cannot all be pursued. This is why coherence making is such an important quality for effective leadership, as we will discuss in Chapter Six. Coherence making, which involves prioritizing and focusing, is greatly facilitated when guided by moral purpose.

Second, and more fundamentally, moral purpose is problematic because it must contend with reconciling the diverse interests and goals of different groups. Diversity means different races, different interest groups, different power bases, and basically different lots in life. To achieve moral purpose is to forge interaction—and even mutual purpose—across groups. Yet the problem is that people are not equal, and the privileged have a vested interest in the status quo as long as it works in their favor.

Still, profit-minded businesses do better when they pay

attention to moral purpose. De Gues (1997) worked for Royal Dutch/Shell for almost forty years and studied "long-living companies." He found that in many countries, 40 percent of newly created companies last less than ten years and that even "the big solid companies" do not hold out for more than an average of forty years (p. 2). By contrast, long-lived companies (those lasting more than fifty years) had a strong sense of purpose and were adaptive to their environments without compromising core ideals.

De Gues (1997) talks about both the negative and the positive case: "Companies die because their managers focus on the economic activity of producing goods and services, and they forget their organizations' true nature is that of a community of humans" (p. 3). In contrast,

> A healthy living company will have members, both humans and other institutions, who subscribe to a set of common values and who believe that the goals of the company allow them and help them to achieve their own individual goals. Both the company and its constituent members have basic driving forces; they want to survive, and once the conditions for survival exist, they want to reach and expand their potential. The underlying contract between the company and its members (both individuals and other institutions) is that the members will be helped to reach their potential. It is understood that this, at the same time, is in the company's self-interest. The self-interest of the company stems from its understanding that the members' potential helps create the corporate potential [p. 200].

Whether we are talking about a biotechnical company or

a school, having moral purpose—both in terms of contribution to society and development of commitment in employees—makes excellent business sense in the middle to long run. Organizations without such purpose die sooner than later. At best, they win the odd early battle and steadily lose the war thereafter.

The message of this chapter is that moral purpose is worthwhile on just about every meaningful criterion; it may not become activated on its own accord, but it is there in nascent form to be cultivated and activated. I have argued elsewhere that moral purpose has a tendency to become stronger as humankind evolves (Fullan, 1999). Thus, in evolutionary terms, moral purpose has a predestined tendency to surface. Effective leaders exploit this tendency and make moral purpose a natural ally. Although moral purpose is natural, it will flourish only if leaders cultivate it.

There are signs that moral purpose is on the ascendency in schools and businesses. A good example is Palmer's *The Courage to Teach* (1998), in which he shows how the best teachers integrate the intellectual, emotional, and spiritual aspects of teaching to create powerful learning communities. With respect to businesses, Garten (2001) interviewed forty prominent men and women around the world who held CEO, president, and chairperson positions in major companies. Garten describes how some executives have made the direct link between social responsibility and the morale, productivity, and loyalty of employees, such as Jarma Ollila, chairman and CEO of Nokia Corporation, whom Garten quotes:

People want their company to be a good citizen. They want it to show true concern for the world, for the environment.

They want it to have a social conscience. There is now a very clear expectation which is coming from political life as well as our employees, that companies will have to have a soul, a state of mind which represents a social conscience. That's very different from the early 1990s when we were applauded just for employing more people. There is a very high expectation, something I did not see when I started as CEO in 1992 [p. 184].

Similarly, Bolman and Deal (2000, p. 185) predict that "culture and core values will be increasingly recognized as the vital social glue that infuses an organization with passion and purpose. Workers will increasingly demand more than a paycheck. They'll want to know the higher calling or enabling purpose of their work."

Garten (2001, p. 192) goes on to say, however, that most leaders "are badly understanding the rise of global problems that will affect their firms and the environment in which they operate. They are failing to see the gap between society's expectations of what they should do and what they seem prepared to do."

The most fundamental conclusion of this chapter is that moral purpose and sustained performance of organizations are mutually dependent. Leaders in a culture of change realize this. Pascale, Millemann, and Gioja (2000, p. 92) found elements of this kind of leadership in the seven companies they studied, and call "sustainability" the challenge of the century: "The theory of sustainability is that it is constituted by a trinity of environmental soundness, social justice, and economic viability. If any of these three are weak or missing, the theory of sustainability says that that practice [what the organization is doing] will not prove sustainable over time."

We are now ready to extend our thinking, because in a non-linear world it is easy to lose one's way, even if one is motivated by moral purpose. If we live in a culture of change—and we certainly do—to understand the change process is a vital quality of all leaders.

Chapter Three

Understanding Change

REMEMBER THAT A CULTURE OF CHANGE CONSISTS OF great rapidity and nonlinearity on the one hand and equally great potential for creative breakthroughs on the other. The paradox is that transformation would not be possible without accompanying messiness.

Understanding the change process is less about innovation and more about innovativeness. It is less about strategy and more about strategizing. And it *is* rocket science, not least because we are inundated with complex, unclear, and often contradictory advice. Micklethwait and Wooldridge (1996) refer to management gurus as witch doctors (although they also acknowledge their value). Argyris (2000) talks about flawed advice. Mintzberg, Ahlstrand, and Lampel (1998) take us on a *Strategy Safari*. Drucker is reported to have said that people refer to *gurus* because they don't know how to spell *charlatan!*

Would you know what to do if you read Kotter's *Leading Change,* in which he proposes an eight step process for initiating top-down transformation (1996, p. 21)?

1. Establishing a Sense of Urgency
2. Creating a Guiding Coalition
3. Developing a Vision and Strategy
4. Communicating the Change Vision
5. Empowering Broad-Based Action
6. Generating Short-Term Wins
7. Consolidating Gains and Producing More Change
8. Anchoring New Approaches in the Culture

Would you still know what to do if you then turned to Beer, Eisenstat, and Spector's observations (1990) about drawing out bottom-up ideas and energies?

1. Mobilize commitment to change through joint diagnosis [with people in the organization] of business problems
2. Develop a shared vision of how to organize and manage for competitiveness
3. Foster concerns for the new vision, competence to enact it, and cohesion to move it along
4. Spread revitalization to all departments without pushing it from the top
5. Institutionalize revitalization through formal policies, systems, and structure

6. Monitor and adjust strategies in response to problems in the revitalization process [cited in Mintzberg et al., 1998, p. 338]

What do you think of Hamel's advice (2000) to "lead the revolution" by being your own seer?

Step 1: Build a point of view

Step 2: Write a manifesto

Step 3: Create a coalition

Step 4: Pick your targets and pick your moments

Step 5: Co-opt and neutralize

Step 6: Find a translator

Step 7: Win small, win early, win often

Step 8: Isolate, infiltrate, integrate

And, after all this advice, if you did know what to do, would you be right? Probably not. Some of the advice seems contradictory. (Should we emphasize top-down or bottom-up strategies?) Much of it is general and unclear about what to do—what Argyris (2000) calls "nonactionable advice." This is why many of us have concluded that change cannot be managed. It can be understood and perhaps led, but it cannot be controlled. After taking us through a safari of ten management schools of thought, Mintzberg et al. (1998) draw the same conclusion when they reflect that "the best way to 'manage' change is to allow for it to happen" (p. 324), "to be pulled by the concerns out there rather than being pushed by the concepts in here" (p. 373). It is not that management and leadership books don't contain valuable ideas—they do—but rather that there is no "answer" to be found in them. Nevertheless, change can be led, and leadership does make a difference.

So our purpose in this book is to understand change in order to lead it better. The list that follows summarizes this chapter's contribution to understanding the change process. As with all five components in Figure 1.1, the goal is to develop a greater feel for leading complex change, to develop a mind-set and action set that are constantly cultivated and refined. There are no shortcuts.

Understanding the Change Process

- The goal is not to innovate the most.
- It is not enough to have the best ideas.
- Appreciate the implementation dip.
- Redefine resistance.
- Reculturing is the name of the game.
- Never a checklist, always complexity.

Before delving into a discussion of each of the items on this list, let's consider Goleman's findings (2000) about leadership that gets results, because they relate to several elements of the list. Goleman analyzed a database from a random sample of 3,871 executives from the consulting firm Hay/McBer. He examined the relationship between leadership style, organizational climate, and financial performance. Climate was measured by combining six factors of the working environment: flexibility, responsibility, standards, rewards, clarity, and commitment. Financial results included return on sales, revenue growth, efficiency, and profitability.

The following are the six leadership styles Goleman identified (2000, pp. 82–83):

1. Coercive—the leader demands compliance. ("Do what I tell you.")

2. Authoritative—the leader mobilizes people toward a vision. ("Come with me.")

3. Affiliative—the leader creates harmony and builds emotional bonds. ("People come first.")

4. Democratic—the leader forges consensus through participation. ("What do you think?")

5. Pacesetting—the leader sets high standards for performance. ("Do as I do, now.")

6. Coaching—the leader develops people for the future. ("Try this.")

Two of the six styles negatively affected climate and, in turn, performance. These were the coercive style (people resent and resist) and the pacesetting style (people get overwhelmed and burn out). All four of the other styles had a significant positive impact on climate and performance.

With this basic introduction to leadership styles, let us now turn to the list items.

The Goal Is Not to Innovate the Most

The organization or leader who takes on the sheer most number of innovations is not the winner. In education, we call these organizations the "Christmas tree schools" (Bryk, Sebring, Kerbow, Rollow, & Easton, 1998). These schools glitter from a distance—so many innovations, so little time—but they end up superficially adorned with many decorations, lacking depth and coherence.

Relentlessly taking on innovation after innovation is Goleman's pacesetter leader (2000, p. 86):

> The leader sets extremely high performance standards and exemplifies them himself. He is obsessive about doing things better and faster, and he asks the same of everyone around him. He quickly pinpoints poor performers and demands more from them. If they don't rise to the occasion, he replaces them with people who can. You would think such an approach would improve results, but it doesn't. In fact, the pacesetting style destroys climate. Many employees feel overwhelmed by the pacesetter's demands for excellence, and their morale drops—guidelines for working may be clear in the leader's head, but she does not state them clearly; she expects people to know what to do.

The pacesetter often ends up being a "lone ranger," as Superintendent Negroni puts it when he reflects on his experience (and on his eventual change to lead learner). During the first three years of Negroni's superintendency in Springfield, Massachusetts, his overall goal was "to change this inbred system": "Intent on the ends, I operated as Lone Ranger. I didn't try to build relationships with the teachers' union or with the board. Instead, I worked around them. Most of the time, I felt that I was way out in front of them. I would change things on my own" (quoted in Senge et al., 2000, p. 426). For all the changes he pushed through, Negroni says, "these were three brutal years for all of us. . . .

I was running so fast and making so many changes that I was getting tired. People around me were even more sick and tired" (pp. 426–427).

Eventually, through reflective practice and feedback, Negroni moved to transforming the district into a learning institution. He explains:

> Our most critical role at the central office is to support learning about learning, especially among principals—who will then do the same among teachers in their schools. At the beginning of the year, three or four central office administrators and I conducted forty-six school visits in forty-six days, with the principals of each school alongside us. Then the administrators and all forty-six principals met together to summarize what we had seen. This is one of a series of walk-throughs that principals do during the course of a school year—with me, with other central office administrators, and with each other. The sequence includes a monthly "grand round," when every principal in the district goes with me and the eight academic directors to spend the day in one school. We break up into subgroups for hour-and-a-half visits, then come back and (still in subgroups) discuss what we saw. Then a representative from each subgroup makes a presentation to all of the principals [quoted in Senge et al., 2000, p. 431].

These principals are still deeply engaged in innovation, but it is less frenetic, more organically built into the culture. Thus pacesetters must learn the difference between competing in a change marathon and developing the capacity and commitment to solve complex problems.

It Is Not Enough to Have the Best Ideas

It is possible to be "dead right." This is the leader who has some of the best ideas around but can't get anyone to buy into them. In fact, the opposite occurs—she experiences overwhelming opposition. The extreme version of this kind of leader is Goleman's coercive leader (2000, p. 82): "The computer company was in crisis mode—its sales and profits were falling, its stock was losing value precipitously, and its shareholders were in an uproar. The board brought in a CEO with a reputation as a turnaround artist. He set to work chopping jobs, selling off divisions and making the tough decisions that should have been executed years before. The company was saved, at least in the short-term." Before long, however, morale plummeted, and the short-term success was followed by another, less recoverable downturn.

Even the more sophisticated versions of "having good ideas" are problematic. Pascale, Millemann, and Gioja (2000) call these leaders *social engineers:*

> Corporations around the world now write checks for more than $50 billion a year in fees for "change consulting." And that tab represents only a third of the overall change cost if severance costs, write-offs, and information technology purchases are included. Yet, consultants, academic surveys, and reports from "changed" companies themselves indicate that a full 70 percent of those efforts fail. The reason? We call it *social engineering,* a contemporary variant of the machine model's cause-and-effect thinking. *Social* is coupled with *engineering* to denote that most managers today, in contrast to their nineteenth-century counterparts, recognize that people need to be brought on board. But they still go about it in a

preordained fashion. Trouble arises because the "soft" stuff is really the *hard* stuff, and no one can really "engineer" it [p. 12, emphasis in original].

But surely having good ideas is not a bad thing. And yes, it is an element of effective leadership, as in Goleman's authoritative style. Goleman (2000) talks about Tom, a vice president of marketing at a floundering national restaurant chain that specialized in pizza: "[Tom] made an impassioned plea for his colleagues to think from the customer's perspective. . . . The company was not in the restaurant business, it was in the business of distributing high-quality, convenient-to-get pizza. That notion—and nothing else—should drive what the company did. . . . With his vibrant enthusiasm and clear vision—the hallmarks of the authoritative style—Tom filled a leadership vacuum at the company" (p. 83).

Goleman's data show that the authoritative leader had a positive impact on climate and performance. So do we need leaders with a clear vision who can excite and mobilize people to committing to it, or don't we? Well, the answer is a bit complicated. For some situations, when there is an urgent problem and people are at sea, visionary leaders can be crucial. And at all times, it helps when leaders have good ideas. But it is easy for authoritative leadership to slip into social engineering when initial excitement cannot be sustained because it cannot be converted to internal commitment.

Put another way, the answer is that authoritative leaders need to recognize the weaknesses as well as the strengths in their approach. They need, as Goleman concludes, to use all four of the successful leadership styles: "Leaders who have mastered four or more—especially the authoritative, democratic, affiliative, and coaching styles—have the best climate and business performance" (p. 87).

Appreciate the Implementation Dip

One of our most consistent findings and understandings about the change process in education is that *all* successful schools experience "implementation dips" as they move forward (Fullan, 2001). The implementation dip is literally a dip in performance and confidence as one encounters an innovation that requires new skills and new understandings. All innovations worth their salt call upon people to question and in some respects to change their behavior and their beliefs— even in cases where innovations are pursued voluntarily. What happens when you find yourself needing new skills and not being proficient when you are used to knowing what you are doing (in your own eyes, as well as in those of others)? How do you feel when you are called upon to do something new and are not clear about what to do and do not understand the knowledge and value base of new belief systems?

This kind of experience is classic change material. People feel anxious, fearful, confused, overwhelmed, deskilled, cautious, and—if they have moral purpose—deeply disturbed. Because we are talking about a culture of pell-mell change, there is no shortage of implementation dips or, shall we say, chasms.

Pacesetters and coercers have no empathy whatsoever for people undergoing implementation dips. They wouldn't know an implementation dip if they fell into it. Effective leaders have the right kinds of sensitivity to implementation. They know that change is a process, not an event. They don't panic when things don't go smoothly during the first year of undertaking a major innovation or new direction. They are empathic to the lot of people immersed in the unnerving and anxiety-ridden work of trying to bring about a new order. They are even, as we shall discuss, appreciative of resistance.

Leaders who understand the implementation dip know that people are experiencing two kinds of problems when they are in the dip—the social-psychological fear of change, and the lack of technical know-how or skills to make the change work. It should be obvious that leaders need affiliative and coaching styles in these situations. The affiliative leader pays attention to people, focuses on building emotional bonds, builds relationships, and heals rifts. The leader as coach helps people develop and invests in their capacity building (Goleman, 2000).

Further, elements of authoritative leadership help. Enthusiasm, self-confidence, optimism, and clarity of vision can all inspire people to keep going. The problems start when you are *only* authoritative or *only* affiliative or *only* a coach. Thus leaders who are sensitive to the implementation dip combine styles: they still have an urgent sense of moral purpose, they still measure success in terms of results, but they do things that are more likely to get the organization going and keep it going.

Redefine Resistance

We are more likely to learn something from people who disagree with us than we are from people who agree. But we tend to hang around with and overlisten to people who agree with us, and we prefer to avoid and underlisten to those who don't.

Not a bad strategy for getting through the day, but a lousy one for getting through the implementation dip.

Pacesetters and coercers are terrible listeners. Authoritative leaders are not that good at listening either. Affiliative and democratic leaders listen too much. This is why leadership is complicated. It requires combining elements that do not easily and comfortably go together. Leaders should have good ideas and present them well (the authoritative element) while at the same time seeking and listening to doubters (aspects of democratic leadership). They must try to build good relationships (be affiliative) even with those who may not trust them.

We will spend more time in Chapter Four taking up the complexities of resistance and its hitherto unappreciated positive side. Suffice it to say here that we need to respect resisters for two reasons. First, they sometimes have ideas that we might have missed, especially in situations of diversity or complexity or in the tackling of problems for which the answer is unknown. As Maurer (1996, p. 49) says, "Often those who resist have something important to tell us. We can be influenced by them. People resist for what they view as good reasons. They may see alternatives we never dreamed of. They may understand problems about the minutiae of implementation that we never see from our lofty perch atop Mount Olympus."

Second, resisters are crucial when it comes to the politics of implementation. In democratic organizations, such as universities, being alert to differences of opinion is absolutely vital. Many a strong dean who otherwise did not respect resistance has been unceremoniously run out of town. In all organizations, respecting resistance is essential, because if you ignore it, it is only a matter of time before it takes its toll, perhaps during implementation if not earlier. In even the most tightly controlled and authority-bound organization, it is so easy to sabotage new directions during implementation. Even when things appear to be working, the supposed success may be a function of merely superficial compliance.

For all these reasons, successful organizations don't go with only like-minded innovators; they deliberately build in differences. They don't mind so much when others—not just themselves—disturb the equilibrium. They also trust the learning process they set up—the focus on moral purpose, the attention to the change process, the building of relationships, the sharing and critical scrutiny of knowledge, and traversing the edge of chaos while seeking coherence. Successful organizations and their leaders come to know and trust that these dynamics contain just about all the checks and balances needed to deal with those few hard-core resisters who make a career out of being against everything—who act, in other words, without moral purpose.

Reculturing Is the Name of the Game

It used to be that governments were the only group constantly reorganizing. Now, with reengineering and mergers and acquisitions, everybody is doing it. And they are getting nowhere. Gaius Petronious nailed this problem almost two thousand years ago: "We trained hard . . . but it seemed every time we were beginning to form up into teams we were reorganized. I was to learn later in life that we tend to meet any situation by reorganizing, and what a wonderful method it can be for creating the illusion of progress while producing confusion, inefficiency, and demoralization" (cited in Gaynor, 1977, p. 28).

Structure does make a difference, but it is not the main

point in achieving success. Transforming the culture—changing the way we do things around here—is the main point. I call this *reculturing*. Effective leaders know that the hard work of reculturing is the sine qua non of progress. Furthermore, it is a particular kind of reculturing for which we strive: one that activates and deepens moral purpose through collaborative work cultures that respect differences and constantly build and test knowledge against measurable results—a culture within which one realizes that sometimes being off balance is a learning moment.

Leading in a culture of change means creating a culture (not just a structure) of change. It does not mean adopting innovations, one after another; it does mean producing the capacity to seek, critically assess, and selectively incorporate new ideas and practices—all the time, inside the organization as well as outside it.

Reculturing is a contact sport that involves hard, labor-intensive work. It takes time and indeed never ends. This is why successful leaders need energy, enthusiasm, and hope, and why they need moral purpose along with the other four leadership capacities described in this book. Later on we will see case examples of reculturing, because it is very much a matter of developing relationships (Chapter Four), building knowledge (Chapter Five), and striving for coherence in a nonlinear world (Chapter Six).

Never a Checklist, Always Complexity

It is no doubt clear by now why there can never be a recipe or cookbook for change, nor a step-by-step process. Even seemingly sophisticated plans like Kotter's (1996) eight steps, or Hamel's (2000) eight, discussed earlier in this chapter, are suspect if used as the basis for planning. They may be useful to stir one's thinking, but I have argued that it will be more productive to develop one's own mind-set through the five core components of leadership because one is more likely to internalize what makes for effective leadership in complex times. This makes it difficult for leaders because they will be pushed to provide solutions. In times of urgent problems and confusing circumstances, people demand leaders who can show the way. (Just try leading by explaining to your board of directors that you have based your strategic plan on the properties of nonlinear feedback networks and complex adaptive systems.) In other words, leaders and members of the organization, because they live in a culture of frenetic change, are vulnerable to seeking the comforting clarity of off-the-shelf solutions. Why not take a change pill, and if that doesn't work, there will be another one next year.

Alas, there is no getting around the conclusion that effective leaders must cultivate their knowledge, understanding, and skills of what has to come to be known as complexity science. (For the latest, best discussion of this subject, see Pascale et al., 2000; and Stacey, 2000; see also my *Change Forces* trilogy, 1993, 1999, forthcoming). Complexity science is one of those remarkable convergences of independent streams of inquiry that I referred to in Chapter One. This science, as Pascale et al. claim, grapples with the mysteries of life and living; it is producing exciting new insights into life itself and into how we might think about organizations, leadership, and social change: "Living systems [like businesses] cannot be *directed* along a linear path. Unforeseen consequences are inevitable. The challenge is to *disturb* them in a manner that approximates the desired outcomes" (Pascale et al., 2000, p. 6, emphasis in original).

The Complexities of Leadership

Leading in a culture of change is about unlocking the mysteries of living organizations. That is why this book places a premium on understanding and insight rather than on mere action steps. Complexities can be unlocked and even understood but rarely controlled.

There are, as can be seen, dilemmas in leading change. Goleman's analysis helps us because it informs us that elements of different leadership styles must be learned and used in different situations. But knowing what to do in given circumstances is still not for sure. If you are facing an urgent, crisis-ridden situation, a more coercive stance may be necessary at the beginning. Those dealing with failing schools have drawn this very conclusion: the need for external intervention is inversely proportionate to how well the school is progressing. In a case of persistent failure, dramatic, assertive leadership and external intervention appear to be necessary. In the long run, however, effectiveness depends on developing internal commitment in which the ideas and intrinsic motivation of the vast majority of organizational members become activated. Along the way, authoritative ideas, democratic empowerment, affiliative bonds, and coaching will all be needed.

In the preceding paragraph I deliberately said that more coercive actions may be needed "at the beginning" of a crisis. This is where leadership gets complicated. When organizations are in a crisis they have to be rescued from chaos. But a crisis usually means that the organization is out of synch with its environment. In this case, more radical change is required, and this means the organization needs leadership that welcomes differences, communicates the urgency of the challenge, talks about broad possibilities in an inviting way, and creates mechanisms that "motivate people to reach beyond themselves" (Pascale et al., 2000, p. 74; see also Heifetz, 1994).

Recall from Chapter Two the case study of the National Literacy and Numeracy Strategy in England. Most people would agree that the public school system is in a state of crisis. It needs authoritative leadership before it disintegrates, but the system is still out of line with its environment, which calls for accelerated change and learning. There can be a fine line between coercive and authoritative leadership. Certainly the strategy in England has elements of coercive as well as pacesetting leadership. Is this degree of pressure required to get large-scale change under way? We don't really know, but I would venture to say that the strategy that moved the English school system from near-chaos to a modicum of success is not the same strategy that is going to create the transformation needed for the system to thrive in the future. For that you need plenty of internal commitment and ingenuity. School systems all over the world, take heed.

The need to have different strategies for different circumstances explains why we cannot generalize from case studies of success. In 1982, Peters and Waterman's *In Search of Excellence* galvanized the management world to inspiration and action. As it turns out, however, of the forty-three excellent companies (and they were excellent at the time), "half were in trouble" within five years of the book's appearance;

"at present all but five have fallen from grace" (Pascale et al., 2000, p. 23).

To recommend employing different leadership strategies that simultaneously and sequentially combine different elements seems like complicated advice, but developing this deeper feel for the change process by accumulating insights and wisdom across situations and time may turn out to be the most practical thing we can do—more practical than the best step-by-step models. For if such models don't really work, or if they work only in some situations, or if they are successful only for short periods of time, they are hardly practical.

We can also see the complexities of leadership in J. B. Martin's comparison of John F. Kennedy and Robert F. Kennedy:

> Jack Kennedy was more the politician, saying things publicly that he privately scoffed at. Robert Kennedy was more himself. Jack gave the impression of decisive leadership, the man with all the answers. Robert seemed more hesitant, less sure he was right, more tentative, more questioning, and completely honest about it. Leadership he showed; but it has a different quality, an off-trail unorthodox quality, to some extent a quality of searching for hard answers to hard questions in company with his bewildered audience, trying to work things out with their help [cited in Thomas, 2000, p. 390].

Robert Kennedy had his ruthless and conspiratorial moments, but it is likely that his style of leadership—committed to certain values, but uncertain of the pathways—is more suited to leading in a culture of change. Being sure of yourself when you shouldn't be can be a liability. Decisive leaders can attract many followers, but it is usually more a case of dependency than enlightenment. The relationship between leaders and members of the organization is complicated indeed, as we will also see in subsequent chapters.

It is time now to continue our practical journey. The next stop is relearning in a different way what we thought we already knew: that relationships are crucial. Of course they are, but what does that really mean in a culture of change?

Chapter Four

Relationships, Relationships, Relationships

IF MORAL PURPOSE IS JOB ONE, RELATIONSHIPS ARE JOB two, as you can't get anywhere without them. In the past, if you asked someone in a successful enterprise what caused the success, the answer was "It's the people." But that's only partially true: it is actually the *relationships* that make the difference.

In pursuing the importance of relationships in this chapter, I will also relate them to the role of moral purpose in business and education. In so doing, I will do something different: let's talk about businesses as if they had souls and hearts, and about schools as if they had minds. We will see that moral purpose, relationships, and organizational success are closely interrelated. We will also find that businesses and schools have much in common. Businesses, as I concluded in the previous chapters, are well-advised to boost their moral purpose—for their own good as well as for the good of society. Schools, particularly because we live in the knowledge society, need to strengthen their intellectual quality as they deepen their moral purpose.

Businesses as If They Had Souls

In "Relationships: The New Bottom Line in Business," the first chapter of their book *The Soul at Work,* Lewin and Regine (2000) talk about complexity science: "This new science, we found in our work, leads to a new theory of business that places people and relationships—how people interact with each other, the kinds of relationships they form—into dramatic relief. In a linear world, things may exist independently of each other, and when they interact, they do so in simple, predictable ways. In a nonlinear, dynamic world, everything exists only in relationship to everything else, and the interactions among agents in the system lead to complex, unpredictable outcomes. In this world, interactions, or relationships, among its agents are the organizing principle" (pp. 18–19).

For Lewin and Regine, relationships are not just a product of networking but "genuine relationships based on authenticity and care." The "soul at work" is both individual and collective: "Actually, most people want to be part of their organization; they want to know the organization's purpose; they want to make a difference. When the individual soul is connected to the organization, people become connected to something deeper—the desire to contribute to a larger purpose, to feel they are part of a greater whole, a web of connection" (p. 27).

It is time, say Lewin and Regine, to alter our perspective: "to pay as much attention to how we treat people—co-workers, subordinates, customers—as we now typically pay attention to structures, strategies, and statistics" (p. 27). Lewin and Regine make the case that there is a new style of leadership in successful companies—one that focuses on people and relationships as essential to getting sustained results.

> It's a new style in that it says, place more emphasis than you have previously on the micro level of things in your company, because this is a creative conduit for influencing many aspects of the macro level concerns, such as strategy and the economic bottom line. It's a new style in that it encourages the emergence of a culture that is more open and caring. It's a new style in that it does not readily lend itself to being turned into "fix it" packages that are the stuff of much management consultancy, because it requires genuine connection with co-workers; you can't fake it and expect to get results [p. 57].

It is time, in other words, to bury the cynic who said "leadership is about sincerity, and once you learn to fake that, you've got it made."

Lewin and Regine then present a series of chapters describing successful businesses that combine a tough commitment to results underpinned by a deep regard for people inside and outside the organization. Examples range from Verifone, the electronic company that increased its revenues from $31.2 million to $600 million in eleven years, to Monsanto, the biotechnology company I discussed in Chapter Two. Lewin and Regine cite Monsanto's main goal, which was to help people around the world "lead longer, healthier lives, at costs that they and their nation can afford, and without continued environmental degradation" (quoted in Lewin & Regine, 2000, p. 208). We saw in Chapter Two that Monsanto, using relationship and caring principles (as well as strategies for activating them), transformed itself from 1993 to 1999, quadrupling share prices.

I also warned in the last chapter: don't generalize prematurely from successful cases. Lewin and Regine leave us with a happy ending with the CEO, Shapiro, talking about Monsanto's awareness of human impact on the environment: "Around *that* [awareness of impact on the environment] coalesced a commitment to sustainable development, which you might describe as finding ways to continue economic growth while not negatively impacting the environment—even *improving* the environment, because that is going to be necessary" (cited in Lewin & Regine, 2000, p. 223, emphasis in original).

We saw from Pascale, Millemann, and Gioja (2000) that Monsanto later faltered because, although it was strongly connected inside, it failed to engage deeply enough with those on the outside. It is still a good company (now merged), but it certainly lost ground. The lesson: never be complacent; reality-test your own rhetoric with outside (and inside) skeptics and dissenters. It is like, say Pascale et al., "walking on a trampoline" (p. 77).

Related to the soul, there is a powerful message from Kouzes and Posner (1998), who discuss "encouraging the heart." At the outset Kouzes and Posner observe that "leaders create relationships" (p. xv). The authors identify seven essentials to developing relationships (p. 18): (1) setting clear standards, (2) expecting the best, (3) paying attention, (4) personalizing recognition, (5) telling the story, (6) celebrating together, and (7) setting the example.

What separates effective from ineffective leaders, conclude Kouzes and Posner, is how much they "really care about the people [they] lead" (p. 149). (You may want to take their twenty-one-item Encouragement Index, pp. 36–37, as one check.)

Other business authors echo the newfounded emphasis on relationships: Bishop (2000) argues that leadership in the twenty-first century must move from a product-first formula to a relationship-first formula; Goffee and Jones (2000) ask, "Why should anyone be led by you?" Their answer is that we should be led by those who inspire us by (1) selectively showing their weaknesses (revealing humanity and vulnerability), (2) relying on intuition (interpreting emergent data), (3) managing with tough empathy (caring intensely about employees and about the work they do), and (4) revealing their differences (showing what is unique about themselves).

Let us now consider some school examples, which focus on developing relationships as essential for getting results. Schools, especially elementary schools, are known for their culture of caring, but can they get tough about bottom-line results? Are they really all that caring if they cannot show that students are learning?

Schools as If They Had Minds

Nothing presents a clearer example of school district reculturing than School District 2 in New York City. Elmore and Burney (1999, pp. 264–265) provide the context:

District 2 is one of thirty-two community school districts in New York City that have primary responsibility for elementary and middle schools. District 2 has twenty-four elementary schools, seven junior high or intermediate schools, and seventeen so-called Option Schools, which are alternative schools organized around themes with a variety of different grade configurations. District 2 has one of the most diverse student populations of any community district in the city. It includes some of the highest-priced residential and commercial real estate in the world, on the Upper East Side of Manhattan, and some of the most densely populated poorer communities in the city, in Chinatown in Lower Manhattan and in Hell's Kitchen on the West Side. The student population of the district is twenty-two thousand, of whom about 29 percent are white, 14 percent black, about 22 percent Hispanic, 34 percent Asian, and less than 1 percent Native American.

Anthony Alvarado became superintendent of District 2 in 1987. At that time, the district ranked tenth in reading and fourth in mathematics out of thirty-two subdistricts. Eight years later, by 1996, it ranked second in both reading and mathematics. Elmore and Burney describe Alvarado's approach: "Over the eight years of Alvarado's tenure in District 2, the district has evolved a strategy for the use of professional development to improve teaching and learning in schools. This strategy consists of a set of organizing principles about the process of systemic change and the role of professional development in that process; and a set of specific activities, or models of staff development, that focus on system wide improvement of instruction" (1999, p. 266). The seven organizing principles of the reform strategy are as follows: (1) it's about instruction and only instruction; (2) instructional improvement is a long, multistage process involving awareness, planning, implementation, and reflection; (3) shared expertise is the driver of instructional change; (4) the focus is on systemwide improvement; (5) good ideas come from talented people working together; (6) set clear expectations, then decentralize; (7) collegiality, caring, and respect are paramount. Elmore and Burney (1999, p. 272) explain:

> In District 2, professional development is a management strategy rather than a specialized administrative function. Professional development is what administrative leaders do when they are doing their jobs, not a specialized function that some people in the organization do and others do not. Instructional improvement is the main purpose of district administration, and professional development is the chief means of achieving that purpose. Anyone with line administrative responsibility in the organization has responsibility for professional development as a central part of his or her job description. Anyone with staff responsibility has the responsibility to support those who are engaged in staff development. It is impossible to disentangle professional development from general management in District 2 because the two are synonymous for all practical purposes.

In 1998, Anthony Alvarado joined Alan Bersin, Superintendent of Public Education San Diego, as Chancellor of Instruction (Chief Academic Officer). A diverse, multicultural, urban district, San Diego City Schools District consists

of 187 schools and 143,000 students. A larger and more complex system than District 2, San Diego had numerous major
innovative initiatives under way during the 1990s, but they
were not integrated or focused. In this respect, San Diego was
typical of many large urban districts that I wrote about in *The
New Meaning of Educational Change* (Fullan, 2001)—lots of
innovative projects that produced pockets of success, along
with an overall situation of overload and fragmentation.

One of the first things that Bersin and Alvarado did was
to restructure the district so that it focused on instruction,
built-in to the line of authority of the system. Prior to their
arrival, the district was organized into five clusters, each su-
pervised by an area superintendent, again typical of large districts. Bersin and Alvarado reorganized the district into first
seven, and then eight families of schools. The area superintendent position was replaced with a new role called "instructional leader." Each instructional leader was responsible for
twenty to twenty-five schools. The expectation was that the
instructional leader would concentrate solely on instructional
leadership (coaching and evaluating principals) and student
performance.

The overall plan is called "Blueprint for Student Success
in a Standards-Based System: Supporting Student Achievement in an Integrated Learning Environment." The emphasis
initially is on literacy and now mathematics, including a number of prevention and intervention strategies designed to identify and correct learning problems early in a child's schooling.
Major investments and procedures have been established that
provide literacy and mathematics materials, and professional
development for all school leaders, staff developers, and peer
coaches. Student achievement is monitored carefully at the in-

dividual, classroom, school, and district levels. A monthly report is issued by the district that discusses and updates strategies being used and progress of the system.

Relationships are carefully coordinated. The most direct manifestation of this are the monthly conferences. The development and support of district and school leaders are carried out in partnership with the University of San Diego in what is called "The Educational Leadership Development Academy." The executive director of the Academy is Elaine Fink, former superintendent and deputy superintendent in New York District 2, who played a major role in the development of District 2 school-based leadership. The eight instructional leaders conduct monthly conferences where their role and performance are continually reviewed. In between meetings the district administration and instructional leaders interact regularly concerning the implementation of instructional practices and student performance. Similarly, each of the eight instructional leaders conduct monthly conferences with their twenty to twenty-five school principals, along with weekly visits and other forms of interaction. The principals in turn have monthly staff conferences with teachers in their schools. All of these monthly conferences are monitored. For example, principal-led staff conferences are videotaped and reviewed by the group of twenty to twenty-five principals. A great deal of individual coaching and daily interactive problem-solving sessions are carried out at all levels.

Like all the case studies of large-scale transformation discussed in this book, interpretation of results is not straightforward. First, I take up the impact on student performance and on the commitment of principals and teachers. District-wide reading results reveal the post-1997 trend. In tests that

Table 4.1.   San Diego City School Districtwide Reading Results.[a]

Year	White	Hispanic	African-American
1993	63.0	35.5	27.0
1994	62.4	35.4	27.0
1995	63.5	36.0	26.4
1996	63.6	35.6	27.4
1997	63.8	34.9	26.1
1998	66.2	39.5	27.9
1999	71.0	42.9	32.7
2000	73.4	45.8	36.7

[a]Percent at or above 50th Percentile
Source: "Districtwide NRT Language Results: 1993-2000." San Diego City Schools, Institute for Learning, Standards, Assessment, and Accountability Program Studies Office.

compare San Diego students with national norms, the percentage of white, Hispanic, and African-American students achieving at or above the 50th percentile is flat-lined in the 1993–1997 period (pre Bersin-Alvarado), and increased incrementally in the 1998–2000 years, as shown in Table 4.1.

What about principal and teacher commitment? It is much like the English National Literacy and Numeracy case discussed in Chapter Two: many teachers and principals objected to the top-down imposition in the first year, but as the strategy began to provide positive teaching experiences and some student results, more and more teachers and principals began to value the initiative. Before hearing from Anthony Alvarado himself, I will consider two external commentaries. The Center for the Study of Teaching and Policy at Stanford University is conducting an ongoing study of the reform. In one survey, principals gave the district high marks for setting expectations, commitment to standards, and focus on teaching and learning. The principal rating of overall district support was 83 percent for elementary school principals, 67 percent for middle schools, and 78 percent for high schools (Stanford University, 2000a).

In a series of interviews with principals and teachers conducted in the 1999–2000 school year, the Stanford researchers made several observations about the status of the reform in its second year, including (1) both principals and teachers overwhelmingly value the new role of principals as instructional leaders; (2) principal leadership and collegial supports have been strengthened across the district; (3) there is more coherence and focus to the district's reform compared with the past; (4) some principals and many teachers object to the top-down way in which the reforms have been introduced; and (5) the vast majority of principals value the content of the reform, and the majority of teachers value it. About a third of the teachers disagreed with the reform, or felt it eliminated other valuable programs (Stanford University, 2000b).

The second external commentary is my own, based on a site-visit in January 2001. In a session with principals, I asked them to respond anonymously to two questions: What were their aspirations or expectations with respect to the reform initiative? What worries or concerns did they have about the initiative? I coded the responses as to whether they were positive, neutral, or negative. Positive meant a strong identity with the goals and content of the initiative, with implementation worries. Neutral or negative indicated a vague notion of the initiative or disagreement with it, or worries that did not relate to the reform itself. I received 166 responses (nearly the full total). Of these, I categorized 135 (81 percent) as positive,

20 (12 percent) as neutral, and 11 (7 percent) as negative. This is just a snapshot, but it is generally consistent with the observation of others—a strong majority of principals endorse the initiative and their new roles.

I also interviewed Anthony Alvarado, who talked about his own sense of progress and intentions:

> We are in our third year. I see and feel that there has been a definite shift to implement the reform. We started with a strong district plan. We wanted to get principals to understand that we have created district parameters. But this initiative is not about simply implementing a district plan. It is about drawing out what principals stand for. Granted, it is not about doing your own thing, but I also don't want principals to follow a procedural plan. I want them to ask "How do I develop a culture in my school that gets people to understand what they can do together to help students?" I am interested in the hearts and minds of principals. The feeling is that something is being done to them, but that is not our intent. We are creating a system for them to take responsibility, for them to understand internally how they can commit deeply to student learning. I actually think that instructional leadership, when it is done well, is transformational leadership. The sense of who I am as a principal or teacher, what I believe in, is ultimately what we are trying to work on. We are trying to create a system to deepen instructional work with a value base that you can stay with because it reflects what you are. I want people to be able to say "What I did was substantial." That "it counted." This deepening of belief is a learning process, and is held together by shared values and beliefs. It requires moral and intellectual attention [Interview, January 29, 2001].

What is happening in San Diego City Schools District is a moving target. It is too early to tell whether the effort will be sustained over many years, and whether its impact will be effective in the long run. On a related matter, in an era of high-stakes testing in schools and with a sense of urgency to show short-term results, leaders in a culture of change require a quality that all long-term effective leaders have—the capacity to resist a focus on short-term gains at the expense of deeper reform where gains are steady but not necessarily dramatic. Unlike businesses that go for immediate profit, schools should resist going for an immediate boost in test scores. As Alvarado recalls:

> When you set a target and ask for big leaps in achievement scores, you start squeezing capacity in a way that gets into a preoccupation with tests, perhaps bordering on cheating. You cut corners in a way that ends up diminishing learning. That is the antithesis of our effort. Whenever we get good data, I want people to prove to me that there is a causal relationship to what we are doing. If I got a 2.5 percent increase every year for ten years, I would be happy. I want steady, steady, ever-deepening improvement [Interview, January 29, 2001].

Bersin and Alvarado demonstrate tough empathy. They clearly focus on learning ("it's about instruction and only instruction"), but they know that principals and teachers will only be mobilized by caring and respect, by talented people working together, and by developing shared expertise. Their leadership is not all that different from the leadership evidenced in the transformed companies such as Monsanto analyzed by Pascale et al. (2000).

Another education example at the level of the school is described in a study by Newmann, King, and Youngs of what makes some schools especially effective. Their latest case studies are most revealing. Newmann et al. (2000) conclude that what they call *school capacity* is the key to success. This capacity consists of five components: (1) teachers' knowledge, skills, and dispositions; (2) professional community; (3) program coherence; (4) technical resources; and (5) principal leadership. The role of these five components in combination is revealing.

The knowledge, skills, and dispositions of teachers as *individuals* is obviously important and can make a difference in individual classrooms. Newmann and his colleagues, however, make the point that this is not sufficient, because the organization must change along with individuals. Thus, professional development or training of individuals or even of small teams will not be sufficient. For this reason schools must also focus on creating schoolwide *professional learning communities*.

Individual development combined with professional communities is still not sufficient unless it is channeled in a way that combats the fragmentation of multiple innovations; that is, there must be *program coherence*, which Newmann et al. (2000, p. 5) define as "the extent to which the school's programs for student and staff learning are coordinated, focused on clear learning goals, and sustained over a period of time." Program coherence is organizational integration.

Another component of school capacity concerns the extent to which schools garner *technical resources*. Instructional improvement requires additional resources in the form of materials, equipment, space, time, and access to new ideas and to expertise. Successful schools are much better at addressing their resource needs.

School capacity is seriously undermined if it does not have the fifth component: *quality leadership*. Put differently, the role of the principal is to "cause" the previous four factors to get better and better. Elmore (2000, p. 15) agrees: "[T]he job of administrative leaders is primarily about enhancing the skills and knowledge of people in the organization, creating a common culture of expectations around the use of those skills and knowledge, holding the various pieces of the organization together in a productive relationship with each other, and holding individuals accountable for their contributions to the collective result."

Look what is being said here. Development of individuals is not sufficient. New relationships (as found in a professional learning community) are crucial, but only if they work at the hard task of establishing greater program coherence and the addition of resources. The role of leadership (in this case, the principal) is to "cause" greater capacity in the organization in order to get better results (learning). Again, there is not much difference from what we have seen in successful business organizations.

As I tout the importance of relationships, this is a good time to enter a word of caution, because relationships are not ends in themselves. Relationships are powerful, which means they can also be powerfully wrong. McLaughlin and Talbert's study of high schools illustrates the nature of good and bad relationships as they affect student learning. McLaughlin and Talbert (2001) conducted detailed case studies of professional learning communities in sixteen high schools. They found that only three of sixteen schools had strong professional learning communities (more about this in a moment) and that some departments within schools had strong communities while others had decidedly weak ones. In one school, for example, "Oak Valley's English department has the strongest technical culture of any department in our sample while the same school's social studies department ranks among the weakest" (McLaughlin & Talbert, 2001, p. 47).

A veteran English teacher at Oak Valley comments: "It's everyday practice that teachers are handing [out] sample lessons they've done, or an assignment that they've tried, and [discussing] when it worked [or] how they would do it differently. Or a new teacher joins the staff and instantly they are paired up with a couple of buddies . . . and file drawers and computer disks and everything are just made readily available" (p. 50). In contrast, teachers in the social studies department speak of "my materials" but never mention their colleagues as resources.

Most revealing is that different teachers as they talk about students reflect radically different assumptions about learning. English teachers' comments are uniformly positive: "We have excellent students, cooperative, and there's good rapport with the teachers." In contrast, a social studies teacher says, "The kids—there's no quest for knowledge. Not all, but that's in general. . . . it's not important to them. They just don't want to learn." Mind you, these are the same students being talked about!

McLaughlin and Talbert sum up the situation in Oak Valley's two departments: "In the social studies department, autonomy means isolation and reinforces the norms of individualism and conservatism. In the English department, professional autonomy and strong community are mutually reinforcing, rather than oppositional. Here collegial support and interaction enable individual teachers to reconsider and revise their classroom practice confidently because department norms are mutually negotiated and understood" (2001, p. 55).

McLaughlin and Talbert show the dramatically different effect these experiences have on the motivation and career commitments of teachers: "When teachers from the Oak Valley English and social studies departments told us how they feel about their job, it was hard to believe that they teach in the same school. Oak Valley English teachers of all pedagogical persuasions express pride in their department and pleasure in their workplace: 'Not a day goes by that someone doesn't say how wonderful it is to work here,' said one. In contrast, social studies teachers, weary of grappling alone with classroom tensions, verbalize bitterness and professional disinvestment. Several plan to leave the school or the profession" (2001, pp. 83–84).

In a wonderfully insightful observation, McLaughlin and Talbert make the point that strong teacher communities can be effective or not depending on whether the teachers collaborate to make breakthroughs in learning or whether they reinforce methods that, as it turns out, do not achieve results. In other words, weak collaboration is always ineffective, but strong communities can make matters worse if, in their collaboration, teachers (however unwittingly) reinforce each other's bad or ineffective practice. This is why close relationships are not ends in themselves. Collaborative cultures, which by definition have close relationships, are indeed powerful, but unless they are focusing on the right things they may end up being powerfully wrong. Moral purpose, good ideas, focusing on results, and obtaining the views of dissenters are essential, because they mean that the organization is focusing on the right things. Leadership, once again, comes to the fore. The role of the leader is to ensure that the organization develops relationships that help produce desirable results.

In the schools McLaughlin and Talbert studied, leadership (or lack of it) at the department or school level (or both) accounted for a large part of the difference in whether strong professional learning communities developed in a way that positively affected student learning. Looking again at Oak Valley's English and social studies departments:

> These very different worlds reveal how much department leadership and expectations shape teacher community. The English department chair actively maintained open department boundaries so that teachers would bring back knowledge resources from district and out of district-professional activities to the community. English faculty attended state and national meetings, published regularly in professional journals, and used professional development days to visit classrooms in other schools. The chair gave priority for time to share each other's writing, discuss new projects, and just talk. . . . English department leadership extended and reinforced expectations and opportunities for teacher learning provided by the district and by the school, developing a rich repertoire of resources for the community to learn.
>
> None of this applied down the hall in the social studies department, where leadership enforced the norms of privatism and conservatism that Dan Lortie [in his classic study of teachers (Lortie, 1975)] found central to school teaching. For example, the social studies chair saw department meet-

ings as an irritating ritual rather than an opportunity: "I don't hold meetings once a week; I don't even necessarily have them once a month." Supports or incentives for learning were few in the social studies department. . . . This department chair marginalized the weakest teachers in the department, rather than enabling or encouraging their professional growth [McLaughlin & Talbert, 2001, pp. 107–108].

Recall that only three of sixteen high schools demonstrated schoolwide professional communities. In comparing effective professional learning communities with ineffective ones, McLaughlin and Talbert talk about the pivotal role of principal leadership:

The utter absence of principal leadership within Valley High School . . . is a strong frame for the weak teacher community we found across departments in the school; conversely, strong leadership in Greenfield, Prospect and Ibsen has been central to engendering and sustaining these school-wide teacher learning communities. . . .

Principals with low scores [on leadership as perceived by teachers] generally are seen as managers who provide little support or direction for teaching and learning in the school. Principals receiving high ratings are actively involved in the sorts of activities that nurture and sustain strong teacher community [McLaughlin & Talbert, 2001, p. 110].

That only a minority of schools and school districts operate in the manner espoused by Alvarado, Newmann et al., Elmore and Burney, and McLaughlin and Talbert is a statement of how very far we have to go in transforming the public school system. Further, that the examples we have looked at are not really examples of transformation but rather preliminary baby steps reveals how deep the necessary cultural change really is.

The point of this section is that schools and school districts can get tough about student learning, can use their minds to identify new and better ideas, and can establish strategies and mechanisms of development. But successful strategies always involve relationships, relationships, relationships.

I have, of course, deliberately reversed stereotypes that portray businesses as needing more soul and schools as needing more intelligence. You could say that businesses should take on the mantle of greater caring and schools should focus on ideas and results, and you would have a point, but this is not the main point.

Where the world is heading (or, more accurately, where it needs to head) makes businesses and schools less different than they have been in the past. Both need to be, and are, increasingly concerned with moral purpose and good ideas if they are to be successful and sustainable organizations. In other words, the laws of nature and the new laws of sustainable human organizations (corporations and public schools alike) are on the same evolutionary path. To be successful beyond the very short run, all organizations must incorporate moral purpose; understand complexity science; and respect, build, and draw on new human relationships with hitherto uninvolved constituencies inside and outside the organization. Doing these things is for their own good, and the good of us all.

It would be the understatement of the year to say that leadership that combines all of the elements just mentioned is demanding. What would be more important in leading in a culture of change—which really means helping people work together when anxiety and related emotions run high—than "emotional intelligence"?

Emotional Intelligence and Resistance

People have always needed emotional intelligence, but in complex times people need it in spades. The culture of change I have been describing is, by definition, rife with anxiety, stress, and ambiguity (and correspondingly with the exhilaration of creative breakthroughs). It should come as no surprise then that the most effective leaders are not the smartest in an IQ sense but are those who combine intellectual brilliance with emotional intelligence.

Goleman (1995, 1998, 2000) has done the foundation work on the topic of emotional intelligence. He cites countless examples and studies, such as the following: "Claudio Ferández–Aráoz, in charge of executive searches throughout Latin America from Egon Zehnder International's Buenos Aires office, compared 227 highly successful executives with 23 who failed in their job. He found that the managers who failed were all high in expertise and IQ. In every case their fatal weakness was in emotional intelligence—arrogance, overreliance on brainpower, inability to adapt to the occasionally disorienting shifts in that region and disdain for collaboration or teamwork" (1998, p. 41). He cites Kevin Murray, director of communications of British Airways: "organizations going through the greatest change are those who need emotional intelligence the most" (1998, p. 42). We are talking, in other words, about *all* organizations that are effective in today's culture.

Goleman (1998) has identified five main emotional competency sets (with several subdivisions), which he divides into the domains of personal and social competence (adapted from table 1, pp. 26–27):

- Personal competence

  Self-awareness (knowing one's internal state, preferences, resources, and intuitions)

  Self-regulation (managing one's internal states, impulses, and resources)

- Social competence

  Motivation (emotional tendencies that guide or facilitate reaching goals)

  Empathy (awareness of others' feelings, needs, and concerns)

  Social skills (adeptness at inducing desirable responses from others)

We have already discussed the four leadership styles that Goleman (2000) found most effective in influencing culture and performance. Underpinning the authoritative, affiliative, democratic, and coaching styles is high emotional intelligence. Low emotional intelligence is the hallmark of coercive and pacesetting leaders.

Stein and Book (2000) have taken these ideas further into conceptualization and measurement in developing the Emotional Quotient (EQ) inventory, which has been administered to more than forty-two thousand people. They say at the outset:

> [E]veryone knows people who could send an IQ test sky-high, but can't quite make good in either their personal or working lives. They rub others the wrong way; success just doesn't seem to pan out. Much of the time they can't figure out why. The reason why is that they're sorely lacking in emotional intelligence. . . .
>
> In everyday language emotional intelligence is what we commonly refer to as "street smarts," or that uncommon ability we label "common sense." It has to do with the ability to read the political and social environment, and landscape them; to intuitively grasp what others want and need, what their strengths and weaknesses are; to remain unruffled by stress; and to be engaging, the kind of person that others want to be around [p. 14].

In a manner similar to Goleman, Stein and Book (2000) name five realms of EQ:

1. Intrapersonal (self-awareness, actualization, independence, and self-regard)
2. Interpersonal (empathy, social responsibility)
3. Adaptability (problem solving, flexibility)
4. Stress management (stress tolerance, impulse control)
5. General mood (happiness, optimism)

Stein and Book warn against the superficial use of EQ and recommend close examination of the strengths needed in certain jobs. Teachers, for example, need to be especially strong on optimism and stress management; in addition, Stein and Book found that teachers who are rigid and lacking in impulse control are ineffective. In their work with the Toronto Maple Leafs, Stein and Book found that independence (one of the subdimensions of EQ) had a reverse effect on sporting success—that is, talented hockey players who went their own way tended to underachieve. In an assessment of the Young President's Organization (comprising CEOs thirty-nine years old or younger), they found high levels of flexibility and independence (which involves listening), which is likely not the precise profile needed to lead larger, more complex organizations.

Need I say much more? If relationships are (almost) everything, a high EQ is a must. And the good news is that emotional intelligence can be learned; in other words, you can improve your EQ by working on it (Stein & Book, 2000; see also Chapter Seven). Effective leaders work on their own and others' emotional development. There is no greater skill needed for sustainable improvement.

In a culture of change, emotions frequently run high. And when they do, they often represent differences of opinion. People express doubts or reservations and sometimes outright opposition to new directions. What about these kinds of resistance? Well, it is not much of an exaggeration to say that leaders in a culture of change welcome it! They certainly reframe it as having possible merit, and they almost always deal with it more effectively than anyone else. Defining effective leadership as appreciating resistance is another one of those remarkable discoveries: dissent is seen as a potential source of new ideas and breakthroughs. The absence of conflict can be a sign of decay. Sometimes, observe Pascale et al. (2000),

prolonged "equilibrium is death" (p. 19). They use many examples which illustrate that allowing (even fostering) negative feedback is a step (not the only one) to needed
improvement. One example is Jack Welch's "workout" at GE,
in which "senior corporate officers were subjected to straight
feedback from the troops in a series of public events. . . .
Welch unleashed a process through which lower-level employees could shine the spotlight of public scrutiny on the most
aggravating bureaucratic policies and redundant work practices" (p. 28). (Warning: don't do this in your own organization unless you have all your EQ faculties intact and
understand the entire process of acting on the results.)

All successful organizations in a culture of change have
been found to a certain extent to seek diversity of employees,
ideas, and experiences while simultaneously establishing
mechanisms for sorting out, reconciling, and acting on new
patterns (see Lewin & Regine, 2000, and Pascale et al., 2000).

This is why I and others have said that investing only in
like-minded innovators is not necessarily a good thing. They
become more like-minded and more unlike the rest of the organization while missing valuable new clues about the future.
By supporting the like-minded, leaders trade off early smooth-
ness for later grief. If you include and value naysayers, noise
in the early stages will yield later, greater implementation.

This is why I endorse Heifetz's seemingly counterintuitive advice (1994), "respect those you wish to silence," and
Maurer's touchstones for "getting beyond the wall of resistance" (1996, p. 54), which include maintaining a clear focus
while you take the concerns of resisters seriously.

I have established in this chapter that the development of
relationships among diverse elements in the organization, in-

cluding those who raise objections, is essential. The next stop on our journey concerns the role of knowledge, another convergence—knowledge sharing fuels relationships. We have already established that relationships are paramount, but did you know that this is largely because they are kissing cousins to the knowledge society?

Chapter Five

Knowledge Building

THE COVER STORY IN THE BUSINESS SECTION OF THE
October 30 *Toronto Globe and Mail* was titled
"Knowledge Officer Aims to Spread the Word" (2000). In its
profile of Rod McKay, international chief knowledge officer
at KPMG, the article said, "McKay's challenge is to get
KPMG's 107,000 employees at all levels worldwide to share
information" (p. M1). "Knowledge sharing," says McKay,
"is a core value within KPMG. Every individual is assessed
on their willingness to share their experience with others in
the firm" (p. M1).

Knowledge building, knowledge sharing, knowledge creation, knowledge management. Is this just another fad? New
buzzwords for the new millennium? They could easily become so unless we understand the role of knowledge in
organizational performance and set up the corresponding

mechanisms and practices that make knowledge sharing a cultural value.

Information is machines. Knowledge is people. Information becomes knowledge only when it takes on a "social life" (Brown & Duguid, 2000). By emphasizing the sheer quantity of information, the technocrats have it exactly wrong: if only we can provide greater access to more and more information for more and more individuals, we have it made. Instead what you get is information glut.

Brown and Duguid (2000) establish the foundation for viewing knowledge as a social phenomenon:

> "Knowledge lies less in its databases than in its people" (p. 121).

> "For all information's independence and extent, it is people, in their communities, organizations and institutions, who ultimately decide what it all means and why it matters" (p. 18).

> "A viable system must embrace not just the technological system, but the social system—the people, organizations, and institutions involved" (p. 60).

> "Knowledge is something we digest rather than merely hold. It entails the knower's understanding and some degree of commitment" (p. 120).

If you remember one thing about information, it is that it only becomes valuable in a *social context*.

> "Attending too closely to information overlooks the social context that helps people understand what that information might mean and why it matters" (p. 5).

> "[E]nvisioned change will not happen or will not be

fruitful until people look beyond the simplicities of information and individuals to the complexities of learning, knowledge, judgement, communities, organizations, and institutions" (p. 213).

Incidentally, focusing on information rather than use is why sending individuals and even teams to external training by itself does not work. Leading in a culture of change does not mean placing changed individuals into unchanged environments. Rather, change leaders work on changing the context, helping create new settings conducive to learning and sharing that learning.

Most organizations have invested heavily in technology and possibly training, but hardly at all in knowledge sharing and creation. And when they do attempt to share and use new knowledge, they find it enormously difficult. Take the seemingly obvious notion of sharing best practices within an organization. Identifying the practices usually goes reasonably well, but when it comes to transferring and using the knowledge, the organization often flounders. Hewlett-Packard attempted "to raise quality levels around the globe by identifying and circulating the best practices within the firm" (Brown & Duguid, 2000, p. 123). The effort became so frustrating that it prompted Lew Platt, chairman of HP, to wryly observe, "if only we knew what we know at HP" (cited in Brown & Duguid, p. 123).

In this chapter, we will see several examples of knowledge-creation and sharing from business and education. These organizations and schools are still in the minority, but they are the wave of the future. (And what we can learn from them dovetails perfectly with the discussion in previous chapters.)

Examples from Business

In their study of successful Japanese companies, Nonaka and
Takeuchi (1995) explain that these companies were successful not because of their use of technology but rather because
of their skills and expertise at *organizational knowledge creation,* which the authors define as "the capability of a company as a whole to create new knowledge, disseminate it
throughout the organization, and embody it in products, services and systems" (p. 3).

Building on earlier work by Polyani (1983), Nonaka and
Takeuchi make the crucial distinction between *explicit knowledge* (words and numbers that can be communicated in the
form of data and information) and *tacit knowledge* (skills, beliefs, and understanding that are below the level of awareness): "[Japanese companies] recognize that the knowledge
expressed in words and numbers represents only the tip of the
iceberg. They view knowledge as being primarily 'tacit'—
something not easily visible and expressible. Tacit knowledge
is highly personal and hard to formalize, making it difficult to
communicate or share with others. Subjective insights, intuitions, and hunches fall into this category of knowledge.
Furthermore, tacit knowledge is deeply rooted in an individual's action and experience, as well as in the ideals, values, or
emotions that he or she embraces" (p. 8). Successful organizations access tacit knowledge. Their success is found in the
intricate interaction inside and outside the organization—interaction that converts tacit knowledge to explicit knowledge
on an ongoing basis.

The process of knowledge creation is no easy task. First,
tacit knowledge is by definition hard to get at. Second, the

process must sort out and yield quality ideas; not all tacit knowledge is useful. Third, quality ideas must be retained, shared, and used throughout the organization.

As Nonaka and Takeuchi (1995) say, "The sharing of tacit knowledge among multiple individuals with different backgrounds, perspectives, and motivations becomes the critical step for organizational knowledge creation to take place. The individuals' emotions, feelings, and mental models have to be shared to build mutual trust" (p. 85).

In further, more comprehensive work, Von Krogh, Ichijo, and Nonaka (2000) subtitle their book "how to unlock the mystery of tacit knowledge and release the power of innovation." Lamenting the overuse of information technology per se, Von Krogh et al. take us on a journey that is none other than an explanation of how effective companies combine care or moral purpose with an understanding of the change process and an emphasis on developing relationships (corresponding, of course, to Chapters Two through Four in this book): "Knowledge enabling includes facilitating relationships and conversations as well as sharing local knowledge across an organization or beyond geographic and cultural borders. At a deeper level, however, it relies on a new sense of emotional knowledge and care in the organization, one that highlights how people treat each other and encourages creativity" (Von Krogh et al., 2000, p. 4).

Knowledge, as distinct from information, "is closely attached to human emotions, aspirations, hopes, and intention" (Von Krogh et al., 2000, p. 30). In other words, there is an the explicit and intimate link between knowledge building and internal commitment on the way to making good things happen (see Figure 1.1 in Chapter One).

I will soon take up the not-so-straightforward chicken-and-egg question of the causal relationship between collaborative work cultures and knowledge sharing, but let's stay for a moment with the conditions under which people share knowledge. Von Krogh et al. elaborate: "Knowledge creation puts particular demands on organizational relationships. In order to share personal knowledge, individuals must rely on others to listen and react to their ideas. Constructive and helpful relations enable people to share their insights and freely discuss their concerns. They also enable microcommunities, the origin of knowledge creation in companies, to form and self-organize. Good relationships purge a knowledge-creation process of distrust, fear, and dissatisfaction, and allow organizational members to feel safe enough to explore the unknown territories of new markets, new customers, new products, and new manufacturing technologies" (p. 45).

Von Krogh et al. (2000) emphasize that a culture of care (certainly not a business term!) is vital for successful performance, which they define in five dimensions: mutual trust, active empathy, access to help, lenience in judgment, and courage. Does this sound like soft stuff better suited to kindergarten? (The courage part is for the teacher.) Not when you see the U.S. Army, KPMG, Gemini Consulting, Monsanto, British Petroleum, Sears, and a host of other companies in "tough" businesses espousing quality relationships as vital to their success.

Many of us have experienced firsthand the consequences of not attending to these matters. Von Krogh et al. (2000, pp. 56–57) summarize Darrah's study (1993) of a computer components supplier.

The company faced severe productivity and quality problems. Management's response was to punish ignorance and
lack of expertise among factory-floor workers; at the same
time, whenever they ran into manufacturing problems, it explicitly discouraged them from seeking help from the engineers who designed the components and organized the
production line. These workers gained individual knowledge
through seizing: They worked on sequentially defined manufacturing tasks and tried to come to terms with the task at
hand, without thinking through the consequences for the
performance of other tasks at other stages of the manufacturing process. When a new worker was employed, he received little training. Yet for productivity and cost reasons,
the novice would be put to work as soon as possible.
Knowledge transactions between workers and engineers
were very rare, and most of the knowledge on the factory
floor remained tacit and individual. The tacit quality of individual knowledge was pushed even farther because the
foremen would not allow personal notes or drawings to help
solve tasks.

Concerned with the severe productivity and quality
problems, a new production director suggested a training
program for factory workers that would help to remedy the
situation. The program was designed in a traditional teaching manner: The product and manufacturing engineers were
supposed to explain the product design and give an overall
view of the manufacturing process and requirements for
each step. At the end of the training session, the engineers
would ask the workers for their opinions and constructive
input—a knowledge transaction intended to improve qual-

ity and communication. The workers, however, knew the consequences of expressing ignorance and incompetence, and they did not discuss the problems they experienced, even if they knew those problems resulted from flaws in product design. Nor did they have a legitimate language in which to express their concerns and argue "on the same level" as the engineers. The workers mostly remained silent, the training program did not have the desired effects, and the director left the company shortly thereafter.

What about the causal relationship between good relationships and knowledge sharing? Most people automatically assume that you build relationships first and information will flow. Von Krogh et al. (2000) seem to accept this causal direction: "We believe a broad acceptance of the emotional lives of others is crucial for establishing good working relationships—and good relations, in turn, lead to effective knowledge creation" (p. 51).

I tend, however, to agree with Dixon (2000). One myth, observes Dixon, is that

> [T]he exchange of knowledge happens only in organizations that have a noncompetitive or a collaborative culture. It follows that the first thing you have to do is to fix the culture and then get people to share. But I have found that it's the other way around. If people begin sharing ideas about issues they see as really important, the sharing itself creates a learning culture. I have, of course, inserted an important caveat in that sentence: "about issues they see as really important."
>
> Ford supplies an illustration of this point. Every Ford plant is responsible for making a 5 percent productivity in-

crease every year. People in the plant refer to it as the "task." This is serious business; as one plant manager said, "If you don't make your task, your successor will." Year after year it is a real chore to keep making the 5 percent task, as production engineers are stretched to find some new process or technique to reduce the cost of labor, materials, or energy. Now, the Best Practice Replication process sends the production engineer in each Vehicle Operations plant five to eight best practices items a week, each of which describes how a sister plant reduced costs. Each item spells out exactly how much was saved, specified in hours, materials, or energy. The production engineers have come to rely on this system as a way to make their task. In fact, on average, 40 percent of task comes from best practices pulled off the system—and in some plants 100 percent of task is taken from the system. It is significant that this system is so well used in an industry that is known for being highly competitive. People use it because the system offers help with a very critical business need. But what has also happened at Ford as a result of this ongoing exchange is a change in the company's culture. A learning culture is developing based on this experiential understanding of why knowledge sharing is important.

It is a kind of chicken-or-egg issue: Which comes first, the learning culture or the exchange of knowledge? Given many organizations' rather abysmal success rate at changing their culture, I would put my money on having the exchange impact the culture rather than waiting for the culture to change [pp. 5–6].

In other words, establishing knowledge sharing practices

is as much a route to creating collaborative cultures as it is a product of the latter. This means that the organization must frame the giving and receiving of knowledge as a responsibility and must reinforce such sharing through incentives and opportunities to engage in it. Recall the words of Rod McKay of KPMG with which I started this chapter. "Every individual is assessed on their willingness to share their experiences with others in the firm" ("Knowledge Officer Aims to Spread the Word," 2000, p. M1).

Von Krogh et al. (2000) draw the same conclusion when they talk about two interrelated responsibilities: "From our standpoint, a 'caring expert' is an organizational member who reaches her level of personal mastery in tacit and explicit knowledge *and* understands that she is responsible for sharing the process" (p. 52, emphasis in original).

Figure 5.1 illustrates the elements of knowledge exchange. Knowledge is constantly received and given, as organizations provide opportunity to do so and value and reward individuals as they engage in the receiving and sharing of knowledge.

The logic of what we are talking about should be clear: (1) complex, turbulent environments constantly generate messiness and reams of ideas; (2) interacting individuals are

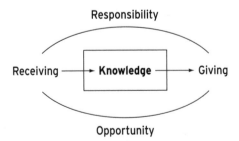

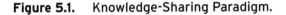

Figure 5.1. Knowledge-Sharing Paradigm.

the key to accessing and sorting out these ideas; (3) individuals will not engage in sharing unless they find it motivating to do so (whether because they feel valued and are valued, because they are getting something in return, or because they want to contribute to a bigger vision).

Leaders in a culture of change realize that accessing tacit knowledge is crucial and that such access cannot be mandated. Effective leaders understand the value and role of knowledge creation, they make it a priority and set about establishing and reinforcing habits of knowledge exchange among organizational members. To do this they must create many mechanisms for people to engage in this new behavior and to learn to value it. Control freaks need not apply: people need elbow room to uncover and sort out best ideas. Leaders must learn to trust the processes they set up, looking for promising patterns and looking to continually refine and identify procedures for maximizing valuable sharing. Knowledge activation, as Von Krogh et al. (2000) call it, "is about enabling, not controlling . . . anyone who wants to be a knowledge activist must give up, at the outset, the idea of controlling knowledge creation" (p. 158). They elaborate: "From an enabling perspective, knowledge that is transferred from other parts of the company should be thought of as a source of inspiration and insights for a local business operation, not a direct order that must be followed. Control of knowledge is local, tied to local re-creation. . . . The local unit uses the received knowledge as input to spark its own continuing knowledge-creation process" (p. 213).

It is important to note that companies must *name* knowledge sharing as a core value and then establish mechanisms and procedures that embody the value in action. Dixon (2000) provides several illustrations:

> One of the best examples . . . is British Petroleum's Peer Assist Program. Peer Assist enables a team that is working on a project to call upon another team (or a group of individuals) that has had experience in the same type of task. The teams meet face-to-face for one to three days in order to work through an issue the first team is facing. For example, a team that is drilling in deep water off the coast of Norway can ask for an "assist" from a team that has had experience in deep-water drilling in the gulf of Mexico. As the label implies, "assists" are held between peers, not with supervisors or corporate "helpers." The idea of Peer Assists was put forward by a corporate task force in late 1994, and BP wisely chose to offer it as a simple idea without specifying rules or lengthy "how-to" steps. It is left up to the team asking for the assistance to specify who it would like to work with, what it wants help on, and at what stage in the project it could use the help [p. 9].

> Probably the best-known example of leveraging knowledge within a team is the U.S. Army's use of After Action Reviews. The AARs are held at the end of any team or unit action with the intent of reusing what has been learned immediately in the next battle or project. These brief meetings are attended by everyone who was engaged in the effort, regardless of rank. The Army's simple guidelines for conducting AARs are (1) no sugar coating, (2) discover ground truth, (3) no thin skins, (4) take notes, and (5) call it like you see it. The meetings are facilitated by someone in the unit,

sometimes the ranking officer but just as often another member of the team. The learning from these meetings is captured both by the members, who all write and keep personal notes about what they need to do differently, and by the facilitator, who captures on a flip chart or chalkboard what the unit as a whole determines that it needs to do differently in the next engagement. Army After Action Reviews have standardized three key questions: What was supposed to happen? What happened? And what accounts for the difference? An AAR may last fifteen minutes or an hour depending on the action that is being discussed, but in any case, it is not a lengthy meeting. . . .

Bechtel's Steam Generator Replacement Group also uses this practice, although it calls the meetings "lessons learned" instead of AARs. Bechtel is a multibillion-dollar international engineering, procurement, and construction company engaged in large-scale projects, such as power plants, petrochemical facilities, airports, mining facilities, and major infrastructure projects. Unlike other parts of Bechtel in which individuals work in ever-changing project teams, the Steam Generator Replacement Group is a small specialized unit that works on a lot of jobs together. Anything learned on one job can be immediately used by the team on the next job. The nature of its work leaves little room for error. The average window of time to replace a steam generator is seventy days or less, unlike the typical Bechtel project, which may last two years or more. This unforgiving schedule mandates that the Steam Generator Replacement Group learn from its own lessons, because even a small mistake can result in a significant delay to a project. The lessons are captured in two ways: first, in weekly meetings to which supervisors are required to bring lessons learned; then, at the end of each project, the project manager brings all players together for a full day to focus on the lessons learned [pp. 37–40].

The design criteria underlying these examples are crucial: (1) they focus on the intended user(s); (2) they are parsimonious (no lengthy written statements or meetings); (3) they try to get at tacit knowledge (this is why personal interaction or exchange is key and why dissemination of "products" or explicit knowledge by itself is rarely sufficient); (4) learning takes place "in context" with other members of the organization; and (5) they do not aim for faithful replication or control.

We could do well enough if we harnessed intracompany knowledge ("if only we knew what we know at HP"). Accessing and creating new knowledge from the outside gets more complicated (see the examples in Pascale, Millemann, & Gioja, 2000). Whether one is promoting intracompany exchanges or accessing external knowledge, the principles are the same: make knowledge building a core value and create specific opportunities to engage in the process. If Shell can do it with 105,000 employees dispersed among 130 "operating companies," we all can do it. In all these cases, there is a need to establish specific procedures and opportunities, such as the "fishbowl" at Shell, described here by Steven Miller, the managing director of the new Oil Products Business Committee (quoted in Pascale et al., pp. 188–189):

One of the most important innovations in changing all of us was the fishbowl. The name describes what it is: I and a number of my management team sit in the middle of a room with one of the country teams in the center with us. The other team members listen from the outer circle. Everyone is watching as the group in the hot seat talks about what they're going to do, and what they need from me and my colleagues to be able to do it. That may not sound revolutionary—but in our culture it was very unusual for anyone lower in the organization to talk this directly to a managing director and his reports.

In the fishbowl, the pressure is on to measure up. . . . If a team brings in a plan that's really a bunch of crap, we've got to be able to call it a bunch of crap. If we cover for people or praise everyone, what do we say when someone brings in an excellent plan? That kind of straight talk is another big culture change for Shell.

The whole process creates complete transparency between the people at the coal face and me and my top management team. At the end, these folks go back home and say, "I just cut a deal with the managing director and his team to do these things." It creates a personal connection—and it changes how we talk with each other and how we work with each other. The country leaders go along because it provides support for what needed to be done anyway. After that, I can call up those folks anywhere in the world and talk in a very direct way because of this personal connectedness. It has completely changed the dynamics of our operations.

The fishbowls, note Pascale et al. (2000, p. 224), are staged for dramatic effect to accomplish work and generate commitment: "The proceedings are videotaped so that when teams return to their operating companies, stakeholders from middle and upper management who were not present at the workshop can watch and learn from the visual record. (These inexpensive videos had a huge multiplier effect on the transformation of Shell's Downstream business.)"

In the same vein, Garvin (2000), after examining several case examples of knowledge-building organizations, summarizes the role of leaders: "First, leaders and managers must create opportunities for learning by designing settings and events that prompt the necessary activities. Second, they must cultivate the proper tone, fostering desirable norms, behaviors and rules of engagement. Third, they must personally lead the process of discussion, framing debate, posing questions, listening attentively, and providing feedback and closure" (pp. 190–191).

Examples from Education

It may seem from the previous pages that business organizations are paragons of knowledge creation and sharing, but it is likely that only a small minority are this good (and they don't necessarily sustain this level of goodness). Many of the same companies appear in different books, so the list seems longer than it actually is. Still, I would say that although the average company is about as bad as the average school system, when it comes to knowledge sharing, the best companies are better than the best school systems. There are proportionately more of them, and they are working more diligently on the task.

It is one of life's great ironies: schools are in the business of teaching and learning, yet they are terrible at learning from each other. If they ever discover how to do this, their future is assured. (Mind you, they are not helped by an oppressive hierarchy that bombards them with multiple colliding demands.)

In Chapter Four I referred to the remarkable improvement of a whole school system in the case of District 2 in New York City under the direction of Superintendent Anthony Alvarado and his staff. We might as well be talking about Shell or Ford as we listen to Elmore and Burney (1999) describe two of the knowledge-sharing strategies employed by the district: intervisitation and peer networks, and instructional consulting services.

Intervisitation and Peer Networks

District 2 [has] a heavy reliance on peer networks and visits to other sites, inside and outside the district, designed to bring teachers and principals into contact with exemplary practices. Intervisitation, as it is called in the district, and peer consultations are routine parts of the district's daily life. Teachers often visit other classrooms in conjunction with consultants' visits, either to observe one of their peers teaching a lesson or a consultant teaching a demonstration lesson. And groups of teachers often visit another school, inside or outside the district, in preparation for the development of a new set of instructional practices. Usually principals initiate these outside visits and travel with teachers.

In addition, principals engage in intervisitations with peers in other schools. New principals are paired with "buddies" who are usually more senior administrators, and they often spend a day or two each month in their first two years in their buddy's school. Groups of teachers and principals working in district initiatives travel to other districts inside and outside the city to observe specific instructional practices.

And monthly districtwide principals' meetings are held on site in schools, and often principals observe individual teachers in their peers' schools as part of a structured agenda for discussing some aspect of instructional improvement. Principals are encouraged to use visits and peer advising as management strategies for teachers within their buildings. A principal who is having trouble getting a particular teacher engaged in improvement might be advised by the district staff to pair that teacher with another teacher in the building or another building in the district. And principals themselves might be encouraged to consult with other principals on specific areas where they are having difficulties.

Intervisitations and peer advising as professional development activities tend to blend into the day-to-day management of the district. The district budgets resources to support about three hundred days of professional time to be allocated to intervisitation activities. Many such activities are not captured by these budgeted resources, since they occur informally among individuals on an ad hoc basis.

A specific example serves to illustrate how professional development and management blend together around peer advising and intervisitation. An elementary principal who is in the last year of her probationary period and is considered to be an exemplar by district personnel described offhandedly that throughout her probationary period, she had visited regularly with two other principals in the district. She is currently involved in a principals' support group that meets regularly with three other principals, and she provides support to her former assistant principal, who was recruited to take over another school as an interim acting principal. In addition this principal has led several groups of teachers from her school to observe teaching of reading and writing in university settings and in other schools in the city. She has attended summer staff development institutes in literacy and math with teachers from her school, and in the ensuing school year, she taught a series of demonstration lessons in the classrooms of teachers in her school to work out the complexities of implementing new instructional strategies. She speaks of these activities as part of her routine administrative responsibility as a principal rather than as specific professional development activities.

Another example of how peer advising and intervisitation models come together in the routine business of the district is the monthly principals' conferences. Most districts have regularly scheduled meetings of principals, typically organized by elementary and secondary levels. These routine meetings usually deal primarily with administrative business and rarely with specific instructional issues. In District 2, in contrast, regular principals' meetings—frequently called principals' conferences—are primarily organized around instructional issues and only incidentally around routine administrative business, and they often take place in the schools. At one recent principals' conference which took place in a school, the meeting principals were asked to visit classrooms, observe demonstration lessons, and use a protocol to observe and analyze classroom practice. Another recent principals' conference convened at New York's Museum of Modern Art. The theme was the development and implementation of standards for evaluating students' academic work. The conference consisted of a brief introductory discussion of District 2's activities around standards by Alvarado; an overview of standards work by the standards coordinator, Denis Levine, and a principal, Frank DeStefano, who has taken a leadership role in developing standards in his school; a series of small group discussions of an article about standards by Lauren Resnick; an analysis by small groups of participants of a collection of vignettes of student work around standards; and an observation of the museum's education programs. Discussion of routine administrative business occupied less than thirty minutes at the end of the seven-hour meeting [Elmore & Burney, 1999, p. 278].

Instructional Consulting Services

District 2 invests heavily in professional development consultants who work directly with teachers individually and in groups at the school site. Over time the district has developed two main types of consulting arrangements. The first type relies on outside consultants, experts in a given instructional area who are employed under contractual arrangements, sometimes with universities and sometimes as independent consultants. The second type relies on district consultants, typically recruited from the ranks of district personnel, paid directly on the district budget, and given an assignment to work in a given instructional area. Principals and school heads play a key role in assessing the needs of the school and brokering consulting services.

The district's first instructional improvement initiative, which began soon after Alvarado's arrival in the district eight years ago, relied exclusively on outside consultants and was focused on literacy, reading, and writing. . . .

Overall the District 2 professional development consulting model stresses direct work by external consultants and district staff developers with individual teachers on concrete problems related to instruction in a given content area; work with grade-level teams of teachers on common problems across their classrooms; consultation with individual teaches who are developing new approaches to teaching in their classrooms that other teachers might use; and work with larger groups of teachers to familiarize them with the basic ideas behind instructional improvement in a given content area. Change in instructional practice involves working through problems of practice with peers and experts, observation of practice, and steady accumulation over time of new practices anchored in one's own classroom setting.

The consulting model is labor intensive, in that it relies on extensive involvement by a consultant with individuals and small groups of teachers, repeatedly over time, around a limited set of instructional problems. Connecting professional development with teaching practice in this direct way required making a choice at the district level to invest resources intensively rather than using them to provide low-impact activities spread across a larger number of teachers. The approach also implies a long-term commitment to instructional improvement in a given content area. In order to reach large numbers of teachers with the District 2 consulting model, district- and school-level priorities for professional development have to stay focused on a particular content area—in this case literacy and math—over several years, so that consultants have the time to engage teachers repeatedly across a number of schools in a year and then expand their efforts to other schools in successive years [Elmore & Burney, 1999, pp. 274–276].

The forms of systematic knowledge exchange in District 2

are being carried on and further developed in the post-Alvarado-Fink period. The reform in San Diego that I discussed in the previous chapter also uses deliberate and focused methods to ensure the development, sharing, and use of knowledge. In addition to "intervisitation and peer networks" and "instructional consulting services," San Diego, as does District 2, makes heavy use of monthly conferences. Recall from Chapter Four that the eight instructional leaders meet once a month with their supervisor, as do the instructional leaders with their twenty to twenty-five principals, as do the principals with their school staff. In all these meetings, the focus is on instruction and associated ideas for developing leadership that will have an impact on teaching practices and student learning.

During my site visit in January 2001, I observed a two-hour session that an instructional leader was conducting with twenty-two school principals. Videotapes of leadership are being used by San Diego more and more to analyze and improve the performance of leaders. In this session, two hours were spent examining a video of one of the principals in the group as she conducted one of the monthly staff conferences with teachers. The principal on tape viewed segments of the video and discussed them with the instructional leader and other principals: Were the purposes and goals of the session clear? Did staff seem engaged? Was there an action-based closure? Was it likely that staff would follow up and do something? And so on. The principal in question was appalled at what she saw: "My goals were not clear," "I can't believe I said what I said," "When I looked at my video there was nothing I could see that was likely to motivate teachers."

As someone observed, "When you look at your own work this way, it is frightening. You are not this charismatic leader. It shakes your foundation." What makes it acceptable is that everyone in the group is videotaped and discussed, including the work of the instructional leader. There must be strong norms of trust and a developmental, risk-taking set of values for these methods to work. When done well, and with integrity, the knowledge sharing in these kinds of settings is phenomenal.

We will see in Chapter Seven how District 2 and San Diego go about recruiting and developing leaders (for example, principals) who can play these more demanding (and more satisfying) leadership roles (see Fink & Resnick, 1999).

Let us take another example. You would think that schools in total know a lot about teaching reading, writing and mathematics—and you would be right. You would also think that accessing this information would be a top priority—and you would be wrong. What is going on here? Well, over the years schools have built up all kinds of structural and cultural barriers to sharing, and they are having a devil of a time overcoming this inertia. (If they weren't so well protected by having nearly a monopoly, and if they weren't so essential to the future of democracy, they would be long gone.) Yet we are finding that teachers and principals, once they experience knowledge sharing, are thirsting for more. They literally can't get enough of it. Let's look at three examples. Carol Rolheiser and I, from the University of Toronto, are working in three school districts: the Edmonton Catholic School District in Alberta, the Toronto District School Board, and the York Region District School Board just north of Toronto.

Assessment for Learning

The Edmonton Catholic School District has eighty-four schools. Working with an internal district steering group, Carol and I are training teams (comprising the principal and several teachers) from all eighty-four schools in four cohorts of twenty-one over a three-year period. This project is called the Assessment for Learning initiative. School teams come together with us for six to eight days per year, during which time they participate in learning about moral purpose, the change process, developing relationships and collaborative work cultures, linking parents and the community, and other topics. As the name of the initiative indicates, the teams focus particularly on what we call assessment for learning, which involves the development of school-based plans to improve student learning. School teams examine how well students are doing, what targets they should set to improve learning, and what strategies might get them where they want to go. They collect data on their own classroom practices and student performance and share these results with other school teams. At each session the groups receive new input and share what they are doing. At the end of a period of development (about a year), we hold a Learning Fair. Its instructions are simple enough to fit on one page: see page 101.

The most recent Learning Fair was held in Edmonton on November 3, 2000. The work produced, the energy in the room, the marvel at what was going on were awesome. Ask anyone who was there. At this event there was a great deal of evidence that ideas discussed in previous group sessions had been put into practice, that new ideas were being generated, and that the culture of the district was becoming more open to examining and sharing its teaching practice. The video that

Learning Fair

. . . an opportunity to showcase, reflect, and celebrate!

The focus of the Learning Fair is to reflect on the successes and challenges of our journey in the Assessment for Learning initiative and to share our learning with each other. The Learning Fair will take place on [date].

Each school is invited to prepare a "storefront" that showcases its leadership work. A storefront is a visual representation of the learning that has emerged from this initiative. You will have the opportunity to discuss your work as other schools explore the storefronts.

The storefront can reflect:

- Concrete actions your leadership team has taken in your school based on the focus of our "Assessment for Learning" initiative
- Artifacts that illustrate the assessment changes in your school
- Successes and outcomes of your work
- Challenges and solutions
- Lessons learned

Tips for preparing the storefront:

- Make sure you have a clearly defined purpose and include the points mentioned above.
- Be creative: think about presentation, color, user-friendly materials. Use a variety of visuals.
- Consider . . . a mind map, a storyboard, artifacts, photographs of work in progress, graphs, charts, products, other
- Include references to any data you generated related to this initiative.
- Prepare an oral description to share . . . no longer than five minutes.
- Provide a one-page summary to accompany your storefront presentation . . . be sure to include the names of your school and leadership team members. This summary should describe key activities and outcomes of your work in Assessment for Learning.
- Setup time will be one hour prior to the fair.

Note: All schools will have the opportunity to present and attend!

was produced from that event could have a tremendous multiplier effect back in the schools and in other districts (provided the principles of knowledge sharing are followed).

Early Years Literacy Project

We are just in the initial stages of the Early Years Literacy
Project (EYLP) in the Toronto District, a large district with
over six hundred schools. We are working with a sizeable
chunk: nine half-days of training over a one-year period with
teams of two from each of the ninety-three schools involved
in the project. Each team consists of the principal and the literacy coordinator (a teacher leader who has a half-time appointment to work with the principal and other teachers on
the improvement of reading and writing in the school). After
just two half-days of training, we asked the 186 participants
to fill out a one-page questionnaire, which included two open-
ended questions: (1) What was the strongest part of the two
days? and (2) What would you like to learn about in future
sessions?

For both questions, the top theme in the responses by principals and literacy coordinators pertained to knowledge sharing. For example, typical responses to the question about the
strongest part of the two days were

- Being able to dialogue with our literacy coordinator
  without the bump and grind of a regular school day
  (principal)

- Discussion with other schools about how they are
  solving some of the issues we are facing at our school
  (literacy coordinator)

- Focusing on what is going on in our school already

(realized there is more going on than I know) (literacy coordinator)

When participants were asked what they wanted in future sessions, their top request involved more dialogue and access to specific ideas:

- Need more knowledge about practice and strategies to make things happen/change in school (principal)
- Would like to hear what others are doing with respect to the [project]—what does it look like, how are they interpreting data to make changes (principal)
- Reflective processes where teachers would reflect on their own personal practices and then relate to the broader picture of what others in the district were doing (literacy coordinator)

We have barely scratched the surface in the Toronto District, but future sessions, including a Learning Fair of accomplishments to date, are designed to go down the path of accessing tacit knowledge and making it available to others in the district.

Performance Plus and Mentor Teacher Project

The third example is the York Region School District just north of Toronto. Here our role is that of external researchers and consultants. The district has commissioned us to document the lessons learned from two initiatives and to make recommendations for future developments. The fifteen most disadvantaged schools in the district are in an initiative called

Performance Plus (focusing on early literacy). Another group, including some of the first fifteen, participate in the Mentor Teacher Project, which provides additional support for teacher development and the improvement of student literacy. Leaders of the projects claim that many schools are experiencing success and that lessons are being learned at the individual level, but *nobody else knows*. The tacit and explicit knowledge being squandered is enormous. Our role is to work with the York region to help it access, understand, and act further on what is already being learned.

In addition to principals and teachers exchanging ideas, we are also working in these projects to involve students in sharing and creating knowledge. They do this within the classroom as they learn to use more powerful interactive learning methods. Students are also taught to present portfolios of their work and accomplishments to their parents. In these ways students are learning why and how to share knowledge—something they will need as future workers and citizens. The more that educators model knowledge sharing themselves in their daily work, the more that students will learn to do so.

As I said earlier, it is ironic that school systems are late to the game of knowledge building both for their students and for their teachers. Most schools are not good at knowledge sharing within their own walls, let alone across schools in the same district. The more general infrastructure for accessing "information" (I use the term advisedly) in national networks and databases is more developed than it is for local networks. Yes, access as much information as you can, but it is the local networks that count, because it is when we are learning in context that knowledge becomes specific and useable. There are a few high-quality regional knowledge-building networks, but even in those situations, intradistrict and intraschool sharing is not strong. Schools systems, in any case, would be well advised to name knowledge sharing as a core value—to label it explicitly, which they do not now do—and to begin to work on the barriers and procedures to dramatically increase its use.

Once again, I conclude that corporations and school systems have much more in common than we thought. They are not identical, but they both would be better off (and hence so would society) if they strengthened their capacity to access and leverage hidden knowledge. And if they do, they will be much better at coherence making in a disordered, nonlinear world.

Chapter Six

Coherence Making

CHANGE IS A LEADER'S FRIEND, BUT IT HAS A SPLIT personality: its nonlinear messiness gets us into trouble. But the experience of this messiness is necessary in order to discover the hidden benefits—creative ideas and novel solutions are often generated when the status quo is disrupted. If you are working on mastering the four leadership capacities we have already discussed—moral purpose, understanding change, developing relationships, building knowledge—you can afford such a friend. You don't have to become Dr. Changelove to realize that living on the edge means simultaneously letting go and reining in.

The ultimate goal in chaotic societies is to achieve greater reining in. It is just that the route to get there is not as linear as most of us would like. The central tendency of dynamic, complex systems—and today's world is certainly an example of such a system—is to constantly generate overload and cause fragmentation. Leaders need to accept this condition as a given, recognize its potential value, and go about coherence making while also retaining the awareness that persistent coherence is a dangerous thing. Fortunately, our mastering the previous four capacities means not only that we can afford to let go but also that we can trust that the dynamics of change, when guided by such leadership, will be conducive to coherence making. Let's see how this dynamic works.

The basis of the new mind-set for leading in a culture of change is the realization that "the world is not chaotic; it is complex" (Pascale, Millemann, & Gioja, 2000, p. 6). The theory (we will get to the practice in a moment) is best summarized in terms of four principles of a "living system," which businesses and schools certainly are (Pascale et al., p. 6; emphasis in the original):

1. *Equilibrium is* a precursor to *death*. When a living system is in a state of equilibrium, it is less responsive to changes occurring around it. This places it at maximum risk.

2. In the face of threat, or when galvanized by a compelling opportunity, living things move toward the *edge of chaos*. This condition evokes higher levels of mutation and experimentation, and fresh new solutions are more likely to be found.

3. When this excitation takes place, the components of living systems *self-organize* and new forms and repertoires *emerge* from the turmoil.

4. Living systems cannot be *directed* along a linear path. Unforeseen consequences are inevitable. The challenge

is to *disturb* them in a manner that approximates the desired outcome.

The Disturbance Part

The key phrase is "disturb them in a manner that approximates the desired outcome." Right away we know that taking on all the innovations that come along or trying to reengineer people is not the kind of disturbance that is going to approximate any desired outcome.

In schools, for example, the main problem is not the absence of innovations but the presence of too many disconnected, episodic, piecemeal, superficially adorned projects. The situation is worse for schools than for businesses. Both are facing turbulent, uncertain environments, but schools are suffering the additional burden of having a torrent of unwanted, uncoordinated policies and innovations raining down on them from hierarchical bureaucracies. Many superintendents (of the pacesetter style) compound the problem with relentless "projectitis." Thomas Hatch (2000, pp. 1–2) shows what happens "when multiple innovations collide": "The list of reforms suggested or attempted since 1983 encompasses almost everything from higher standards and new tests for student performance to merit pay and school-based management. . . . And it is not uncommon now to find school districts in which vastly different approaches to educational reform are being attempted at the same time. . . . In fact, in a study of 57 different districts from 1992–1995, Hess (1999) reports that the typical urban district pursued more than eleven 'significant initiatives' in basic areas such as rescheduling, curriculum, assessment, professional development and school management." Hatch further states, "As a result, rather than contributing to substantial improvements, adopting improvement programs may also add to the endless cycle of initiatives that seem to sap the strength and spirit of schools and their communities" (p. 4).

In a survey of schools in districts in California and Texas, Hatch (2000) reports that 66 percent of the schools were engaged with three or more improvement programs, 22 percent with six or more; and in one district, 19 percent of the schools "were working with nine or more different improvement programs simultaneously" (p. 9).

The result, according to one associate superintendent, is that "frustration and anger at the school level have never been higher. When attempting to garner new funds or develop new programs, over and over again, he [the associate superintendent] hears from principals and teachers 'we don't want anything else. We're over our heads'" (Hatch, 2000, p. 10). One external provider reported, "We work in schools that have seven, eight, nine, affiliations with outside organizations all purporting to have something to do with reform" (p. 25).

The situation Hatch describes is not what I mean by disturbance. Productive disturbance is likely to happen when it is guided by moral purpose and when the process creates and channels new tensions while working on a complex problem. Because the most interesting problems are complex and because there can be no advance blueprint for such cases, Heifetz (1994) says we need adaptive leadership, or, as the title of his book suggests, leadership without easy answers.

When the situation is complex, effective leaders sometimes tweak the status quo even when clear solutions are not evident. Earlier in this book we saw how Shapiro at Monsanto "disturbed" the system through "town hall meetings" that unleashed a process of dialogue among rank-and-file members (Chapter Two); how Alvarado, in School District 2 and in San Diego, created anxiety by focusing intensely on instruction and student performance data that had to be acted on (Chapter Four); and how Welch at GE invited employee scrutiny of existing practices in so-called workout sessions (Chapter Four).

I have to say that top-down, blueprinted strategies or reengineering or relentless innovativeness all turn out to be more reckless than the disturbances we are talking about in the examples in this book. Recall the "fishbowl" technique used by Steve Miller of Shell (as described in Chapter Five), through which people in the organization have an opportunity to observe and critique plans being proposed. Pascale et al. (2000) report on Miller's reflection about the set of new processes used at Shell:

> Top-down strategies don't win too many ball games today. Experimentation, rapid learning, seizing the momentum of success works better. We needed a different definition of strategy and a different way to generate it. In the past, strategy was the exclusive domain of the CMD [Shell's chairman and his team]. But in the multi-front war Shell was engaged in, the top can't possibly have all the answers. The leaders provide the vision and are the context setters. But the actual solutions about how best to meet the challenges of the moment—those thousands of strategic challenges encountered every day—have to be made by the people closest to the action—the people at the coal face. Everyone and everything is affected.

Change your approach to strategy and you change the way a company runs. The leader becomes a context setter, the designer of a learning experience—not an authority figure with solutions. Once the folks at the grassroots realize they own the problem, they also discover that they can help create and own the answer—and they get after it very quickly, very aggressively, and very creatively, with a lot more ideas than the old-style strategic direction could ever have prescribed from headquarters. It worked because the people at the coal face usually know what's going on. They see the competitive threats and our inadequate response every day. Once you give them the context, they can do a better job of spotting opportunities and stepping up to decisions. In less than two years, we've seen astonishing progress in our retail business in some twenty-five countries. This represents around 85 percent of our retail sales volume and we have now begun to use this approach in our service organizations and lubricant business.

A program like this is a high-risk proposition, because it goes counter to the way most senior executives spend their time. When I began spending 50 to 60 percent of my time at this (with no direct guarantee that what I was doing would make something happen down the line), I raised a lot of eyebrows. People want to evaluate this against the old way which gives you the illusion of "making things happen." I encountered lots of thinly veiled skepticisms: "Did your net income change from last quarter because of this change process?" These challenges create anxiety. The temptation, of course, is to reimpose your directives and controls even though we had an abundance of proof that this would not work. The grassroots approach to strategy development and implementation doesn't happen overnight. But it does happen. People always want results yesterday. But the process and behavior that drive authentic strategic change aren't like that.

It's like becoming the helmsman of a big ship when you've grown up behind the steering wheel of a car. This approach isn't about me. It's about rigorous, well-taught marketing concepts, combined with a strong design, that enable frontline employees to think like businesspeople. Top executives and frontline employees learn to work together in partnership.

There's another kind of risk to the leaders of a strategic inquiry of this kind—and that's the risk of exposure. You're working very closely and intensely with all levels of staff, and they get to assess and evaluate you directly. Before, you were remote from them; now, you're very accessible. If that evaluation comes up negative, you've got a big-time problem.

Finally, the scariest part is letting go. You don't have the same kind of control that traditional leadership is used to. What you don't realize until you do it is that you may, in fact, have more control—but in a different fashion. You get more feedback than before, you learn more than before, you know more through your own people about what's going on in the marketplace and with customers than before. You still have to let go of the old sense of control [quoted in Pascale et al., 2000, pp. 191–192].

Remember from Figure 1.1 in Chapter One that the route to making more good things happen and preventing more bad things from occurring is a process that generates widespread internal commitment from members of the organization. You can't get there from here without amplifying and working through the discomfort of disturbances. When change occurs, there will be disturbances, and this means that there will be differences of opinion that must be reconciled. Effective leadership means guiding people through the differences and, indeed, enabling differences to surface.

If the notion of enabling disturbances disturbs you, you don't have to be this radical. Working on coherence making directly is not a bad idea in a world that is loaded with uncertainty and confusion. But you do need to go about coherence making by honoring the change guidelines in previous chapters, which in effect require differences about the nature and direction of change to be identified and confronted. This is so because the only coherence that counts is not what is on paper nor what top management can articulate, but what is in the minds and hearts of members of the organization. Rest assured also that the processes embedded in pursuing moral purpose, the change process, new relationships, and knowledge sharing, do actually produce greater and deeper coherence as they unfold.

The Coherence-Making Part

There are two concepts in complexity science that relate to the coherence-making role, namely, self-organizing and strange attractors. *Self-organizing* concerns new patterns of relationship and action that emerge when you set up the conditions and processes described in Chapters Two through Five. When you do this the dynamics are such that the organization shifts to a new state *as a result of the new interactions and ideas.* Such new states represent breakthroughs in which greater coherence is achieved. This, I hope it is clear, is absolutely not a leaderless proposition. Leaders in a culture of change deliberately establish innovative conditions and processes (again, as in Chapters Two through Five) in the first place, and they guide them after that. Leaders are actually more influential on the ground in this scenario than they are with traditional, more (seemingly) control-based strategies. Pascale et al. (2000, p. 175) advise these new leaders to "design more than engineer, discover more than dictate, and decipher more than presuppose."

Strange attractors involve experiences or forces that attract the energies and commitment of employees. They are strange because they are not predictable in a specific sense, but as outcomes are likely (if not inevitable) in the processes we are describing. Think of a strange attractor as a series of experiences that will galvanize (attract) the deep energies and commitment of organization members to make desirable things happen. Visions, for example, can act as attractors, but only when they are shared at all levels of the organization, and only when they emerge through experience, thereby generating commitment. By contrast, lofty visions crafted in the boardroom or on a retreat meet the "strange" criterion in the eyes of employees, but not the "attractor" one. (I like the superintendent in Susan Moore Johnson's study [1996] who said, "Ten years ago if I'd had a vision they would have locked me up and now I can't get a job without one.") Charismatic leaders can also be strange attractors, but, as I mentioned in Chapter One, they generate short-term external commitment at best, and at worst, dangerous dependency. In his study of gurus, psychiatrist Anthony Storr (1997) warns us that charismatic leaders often function as a seductive trap to solve the chaos we feel in complex times. What disciples get out of the relationship, he says, is the comfort of having someone else take responsibility for their decisions; "the charisma of certainty is a snare, which entraps the child who is latent in us all" (p. 233). Effective strange attractors, on the other hand, possess the magnetic luring power of exploring moral purpose through a series of change experiences, supported by collaborative relationships, that generate and sort out new knowledge.

We can see this process at work in the District 2 and San Diego case studies. Alvarado and his team raise the moral stakes by stressing "we are about instruction and only instruction" in the service of student learning. Had he declared only this, like so many other superintendents, the experience would have been one more ho-hum, "this too shall pass" phenomenon for the principals and teachers. But he also proceeded to design (not dictate) means of pursuing this goal through intervisitation and peer networks, instructional consulting services, and the like, which were bound to produce "attractors" (new solutions) that could be pulled out, reinforced, and built upon.

When I say disturbance is a good thing, I am not against coherence, but in fact just the opposite: unsettling processes provide the best route to greater all-round coherence. In other words, the most powerful coherence is a function of having worked through the ambiguities and complexities of hard-to-solve problems. The leader's coherence-making capacity, in this sense, is a matter of timing. There is a time to disturb and a time to cohere. Good leaders attack incoherence when it is a function of random innovativeness or prolonged confusion.

Perhaps it is time to reassure those who are uneasy with the proposition that allowing, even fostering, disturbances is a responsible thing to do in perilous times. (I hope you have been persuaded to abandon the have-a-great-vision-and-implement-it strategy.) This is a time to emphasize that there is a great deal of coherence making in Figure 1.1 from start to finish. Moral purpose sets the context; it calls for people to aspire to greater accomplishments. The standards in relation to outcomes can be very high indeed, as they are in the cases cited in this book. These standards are also a reverse-driver for achieving coherence. For example, in education, in our work on school improvement my colleagues and I have developed the idea that greater "assessment literacy" is crucial. We define assessment literacy as consisting of

- The capacity of teachers and principals to examine student performance data and make critical sense of them (to know good work when they see it, to understand achievement scores [for example, concerning literacy], to disaggregate data to identify subgroups that may be disadvantaged or underperforming)

- The capacity to develop action plans based on the understanding gained from the aforementioned data analysis in order to increase achievement

- The corresponding capacity to contribute to the political debate about the uses and misuses of achievement data in an era of high-stakes accountability

In sum, through focusing on outcomes (what students are learning), assessment literacy is a powerful coherence-maker. Focusing on outcomes clarifies for teachers and principals what they are trying to accomplish and drives backward through the process toward moral purpose. It helps schools produce more coherent action plans.

This moral purpose–outcome combination won't work if we don't respect the messiness of the process required to identify best solutions and generate internal commitment from the majority of organization members. Within the apparent disorder of the process there are hidden coherence-making features. The first of these features is what can be called lateral accountability. In hierarchical systems, it is easy to get away with superficial compliance or even subtle sabotage. In the interactive system I have been describing, it is impossible to get away with not being noticed (similarly, good work is more easily recognized and celebrated). There is, in fact, a great deal of peer pressure along with peer support in collaborative organizations. If people are not contributing to solutions, their inaction is more likely to stand out. The critical appraisal in such systems, whether it be in relation to the performance of a peer or the quality of an idea, is powerful.

A second coherence-making feature concerns the sorting process embedded in the knowledge-creation and knowledge-sharing activities described in Chapter Five. The criteria for retaining an idea are (1) Does it work? and (2) Does it feed into our overall purpose? Knowledge sharing, in effect, comprises a continuous, coherence-making sorting device for the organization.

The third feature involves the shared commitment to selected ideas and paths of action. People stimulate, inspire, and motivate each other to contribute and implement best ideas, and best ideas mean greater overall coherence.

In short, highly interactive systems with moral purpose

have great cohesive powers built in; with such powers in place, what we have left to worry about are complacency, blind spots, and groupthink, so we thus seek new diversity and new disturbances. And so the cycle goes.

We have come on a pretty complicated journey. I have said that leadership in a culture of change requires a new mind-set that serves as a guide to day-to-day organization development and performance. We obtained, I hope, a good sense of what the mind-set consists of and a good sense of how it plays itself out in actual cases from businesses and school systems. But how do leaders get this good? The answer is, "by learning in organizations like the ones I described." Tautologies aside, developing leaders for a culture of change involves slow learning over time. Rapid change, slow learning—a paradox that brings us to the hare and the tortoise.

Chapter Seven

The Hare and the Tortoise

N FONTAINE'S FABLE, THE HARE IS QUICK, CLEVER, HIGH on hubris, and a loser. The tortoise is slow and purposeful; he adapts to the terrain and is a winner. I admit that the tortoise's way is not perfectly analogous to leading in a culture of change, because if the tortoise had known about complexity science, it might have engaged in a creative diversion or two. Still, the tortoise won, and people, like tortoises, have to stick their necks out to get somewhere.

The lessons for developing leaders in a culture of change are more tortoise-like than hare-like because they involve slow learning in context over time. What are these lessons? In this book, we have learned three powerful lessons about leadership that have implications for developing more of it. Fortunately, they are intricately interrelated: the vital and paradoxical need for slow knowing, the importance of learning in context, and the need for leaders at all levels of the organization, in order to achieve widespread internal commitment.

Slow Knowing

When talking about leading on the edge of chaos, it may seem odd to say that what Claxton (1997) calls *slow knowing* becomes more important rather than less. Claxton provides the reason: "Recent scientific evidence shows convincingly that the more patient, less deliberate modes are particularly suited to making sense of situations that are intricate, shadowy or ill defined" (p. 3).

In other words, under conditions of complex, nonlinear evolution, we need more slow knowing. "Hare brained" is about chasing relentless innovation; "tortoise mind" is about absorbing disturbances and drawing out new patterns. Entirely consistent with our previous chapter, Claxton (1997, p. 214) observes:

> Those who try to manage nations and corporations—ministers and executives of all persuasions—may be panicked by the escalating complexity of the situations they are attempting to control into assuming that time is the one thing they have not got. Their fallacy is to suppose that the faster things are changing, the faster and more earnestly one has to think. Under this kind of pressure [they] may be driven to adopt one shallow nostrum, one fashionable idea after another, each turning out to have promised more than it was capable of delivering. Businesses are re-engineered, hierarchies are flattened, organisations try to turn themselves into *learning* organisations, companies become "virtual." Meetings pro-

liferate; the working day expands; time gets shorter. So much time is spent processing information, solving problems and meeting deadlines that there is none left in which to think. Even "intuitive thinking" itself can easily become yet another fad that fails—because the underlying mindset hasn't changed [p. 214].

In referring to "hard cases" (situations of complexity), Claxton says, "One needs to be able to soak up experience of complex domains—such as human relationships—through one's pores, and to extract subtle, contingent patterns that are latent within it. And to do that one needs to be able to attend to a whole range of situations patiently without comprehension; to resist the temptation to foreclose on what that experience may have to teach" (1997, p. 192).

Claxton talks about the poet John Keats's reference to "negative capability," which is the capacity to "cultivate the ability to wait—to remain attentive in the face of incomprehension" (1997, p. 174). In my lexicon, remaining attentive is to have moral purpose; incomprehension is to respect the complexities of situations that do not have easy answers. Claxton continues, "To wait in this kind of way requires a kind of inner security; the confidence that one may lose clarity and control without losing one's self. Keats's description of negative capability came in a letter to one of his brothers, following an evening spent in discussion with his friend Charles Dilke—a man who, as Keats put it, could not 'feel he had a personal identity unless he had made up his mind about everything'" (p. 174).

Beware of leaders who are always sure of themselves. Effective leaders listen attentively—you can almost hear them listening. Ineffective leaders make up their minds prematurely and, by definition, listen less thereafter. I recall a high-ranking civil servant who said about his boss, "His problem is that he is so bright that he stops listening as soon as he has understood the point." Not a very good way to build relationships or to pick up ideas that you might have missed.

Paradoxically, slow knowing doesn't have to take a long time. It is more of a disposition that can be "acquired and practised" (Claxton, 1997, p. 214). Again, effective leaders seem to understand this. They see the bigger picture; they don't panic when things go wrong in the early stages of a major change initiative. It is not so much that they take their time, but rather that they know it takes time for things to gel. If they are attentive to the five leadership capacities in this book, they know things are happening all the time, even when there is not closure. In a sense, they take as much time as the situation will allow, and do not rush to conclusions in order to appear decisive.

To get this good itself requires time. Conger and Benjamin (1999, p. 262) suggest a ten-year rule of thumb "as the threshold time for individuals . . . to attain the status of expert." But we all know the difference between ten years of experience and one year of experience ten times over. Therefore, the experience must be intensive and must constantly cultivate the capacity to hone one's moral purpose and knowledge of nonlinear change processes, to build relationships with diverse groups, to build knowledge, and to strive for coherence. Most organizations do not function in a manner that provides these kinds of learning experiences—just the opposite in some ways: they teach people to get better at a bad game (Block, 1987). And, as tempting as it is to try, we have also learned that it is not sufficient to package this knowledge and try to teach it. For many reasons, it must be learned *in context.*

Learning in Context

A second lesson is that learning in context over time is essential. Let us be precise here because aspects of this lesson are counterintuitive. Attempting to recruit and reward good people is helpful to organizational performance, but it is not the main point. Providing a good deal of training is useful, but that too is a limited strategy. Elmore (2000) tells us why focusing only on talented individuals will not work:

> What's missing in this view [focusing on talented individuals] is any recognition that improvement is more of a function of *learning to do the right thing in the setting where you work* than it is of what you know when you start to do the work. Improvement at scale is largely a *property of organizations,* not of the pre-existing traits of the individuals who work in them. Organizations that improve do so because they create and nurture agreement on what is worth achieving, and they set in motion the internal processes by which people progressively learn how to do what they need to do in order to achieve what is worthwhile. Importantly, such organizations select, reward and retain people based on their willingness to engage the purposes of the organization and to acquire the learning that is required to achieve those purposes. Improvement occurs through organized social learning. . . .
>
> Experimentation and discovery can be harnessed to social learning by connecting people with new ideas to each other in an environment in which ideas are subject to

scrutiny, measured against the collective purposes of the organization, and tested by the history of what has already
been learned and is known [p. 25, emphasis in original ex-
cept for "in the setting where you work"].

This is a fantastic insight: learning in the setting where you
work, or learning in context, is the learning with the greatest
payoff because it is more specific (customized to the situation)
and because it is social (involves the group). Learning in context is developing leadership and improving the organization
as you go. Such learning changes the individual and the context simultaneously.

We can return to District 2 in New York City and to the
San Diego district to see what learning in context means. The
leadership in these districts considers the development of
school principals as the key to school success (think of the
principal as a branch plant manager). The single most important factor ensuring that all students meet performance goals
at the site level is the leadership of the principal—leadership
being defined as *the guidance and direction of instructional
improvement.*" Focusing on selecting principals who are in-
structionally focused is a necessary first step, followed by creating an intense, comprehensive system of professional
development to promote their continued growth. Comprehensive training for principals would include on-site coaching
of the strategies and behaviors that principals need to utilize
with their teachers in their classrooms to improve the learning of their students.

Opportunities to learn through study groups, action research, and the sharing of experiences in support groups create real supports for principals so that the complicated and

difficult problems of instructional leadership can be addressed. High performing districts utilize a monthly principals' conference as a leadership development tool. This conference is jointly planned and evaluated, and creates a forum for common learning, critique, collegial sharing, and the development of a powerful culture of mutual support. "Buddy" principals (regular cross-team visitations)—opportunities for mentoring where principals are released full-time to serve as mentors or remain in their assignment ("sitting" principals) while mentoring—offer practicing principals the opportunity to work deeply on the skills and behaviors that require continuous coaching. Successful districts annually increase their investment in principal training in order to broaden and deepen the array of leadership strategies that their site leaders possess (Fullan, Alvarado, Bridges, & Green, 2000, pp. 9–10).

The number of organizational practices in District 2 that involve principals' "learning in context" is impressive. These practices include:

- *Intervisitation* Regularly scheduled visits of principals to schools throughout the district to view implementation of initiatives

- *Monthly Principal Support Groups* Monthly conferences with district instructional leaders and other principals to discuss strategies, progress toward goals, and the like

- *Principal Peer Coaching* Full-time mentor principals and selected sitting principals coach individual principals on a regular basis

- *Supervisory Walkthrough* On-site visits by supervisors to address individual needs of schools and to provide guidance to principals

- *District Institutes* Institutes on topics such as literacy, mathematics, standards, and assessment

- *Principals' Study Groups* Groups investigating preselected content areas or a problem of practice which is investigated

- *Individualized Coaching* One-to-one coaching for individual principals, including all newly appointed principals, led by district superintendent or principal mentors

The rationale underlying these practices and additional examples are described in Fink and Resnick (1999). The goal is to develop leaders at all levels who focus intensely on instruction and learning. Fink and Resnick (p. 5) emphasize that "the principal in a District 2 school is responsible for establishing a *culture of learning* in the school, one in which questions of teaching and learning provide the social life and interpersonal relations of those working in the school" (emphasis in original).

These learning-to-lead practices continue to be refined in the work of the Leadership Academy in San Diego. The Academy has been established in partnership with the University of San Diego. The purpose of the academy is "to comprehensively address the recruitment and development of high-quality educational leadership at all levels of the system" (The Leadership Academy at University of San Diego, 2000). The Leadership Academy goals are specifically defined as:

1.   Identify practitioners who have demonstrated knowledge and skill in teaching and learning, and create a newly designed certification program of theory and practice that will truly prepare graduates for the challenges of site-based leadership. University professors and outstanding leaders from San Diego City Schools, together, will develop a rigorous curriculum that incorporates the best leadership research with a full time internship under the guidance of an outstanding principal.

2.   Design and implement a program for the development of district leadership with the eight instructional leaders of San Diego City Schools. This work will include training in the development of powerful principal work plans, the design and execution of highly effective principal conferences, and the improvement of coaching skills utilized during school visits.

3.   Provide training and support in the improvement of principal professional development. This work addresses the quality of the principal mentoring initiative, study groups, focused school leadership, interschool and interdistrict visitation, principals' professional development, and content learning and summer seminars and courses for further study [The Leadership Academy, 2000].

With the practices just described, if you are a principal in District 2 or in San Diego, you can't help but learn to become a better leader and to foster leadership in others. In another publication, Elmore (2000) makes explicit the reasoning underlying these practices while lamenting the absence of such conditions in most school systems (and, we could easily add, in most organizations).

Unfortunately the existing system doesn't value continuous learning as a collective good and does not make this learning the individual and social responsibility of every member of the system. Leadership must create conditions that value learning as both an individual and collective good. Leaders must create environments in which individuals expect to have their personal ideas and practices subjected to the scrutiny of their colleagues, and in which groups expect to have their shared conceptions of practice subjected to the scrutiny of individuals. Privacy of practice produces isolation; isolation is the enemy of improvement.

Learning requires modeling: Leaders must lead by modeling the values and behavior that represent collective goods. Role-based theories of leadership wrongly envision leaders who are empowered to ask or require others to do things they may not be willing or able to do. But if learning, individual and collective, is the central responsibility of leaders, then they must be able to model the learning they expect of others. Leaders should be doing, and should be seen to be doing, that which they expect or require others to do. Likewise, leaders should expect to have their own practice subjected to the same scrutiny as they exercise toward others [pp. 20–21].

All through this book the message has been that organizations transform when they can establish mechanisms for learning in the dailiness of organizational life. As Elmore (2000) puts it, "People make . . . fundamental transitions by having *many* opportunities to be exposed to ideas, to argue them to their own normative belief systems, to practice the behaviors that go with those values, to observe others practicing those behaviors, and, most importantly, to be successful at practicing in the presence of others (that is, to be seen to be successful). In the panoply of rewards and sanctions that attach to accountability systems, the most powerful incentives reside in the face-to-face relationships among people in the organization, not in external systems" (p. 31).

Leaders in a culture of change create these conditions for daily learning, and they learn to lead by experiencing such learning at the hands of other leaders. Leaders are not born; they are nurtured.

We can now see why the knowledge-sharing practices described in Chapter Five *are* learning in context. Peer Assist, After Action Learning, the fishbowl, best practices, lessons learned, the Learning Fair, intervisitation—all have the quality of learning on the spot, or at least very soon after the spot. They involve learning here and now so that the next time will be better. The techniques are important, but they work only when leaders understand the deep cultural values that underpin them. Incidentally, learning in context itself is an exercise in getting at tacit knowledge. It doesn't do much good and may in fact be harmful to start using the techniques as products—that is, as ends in themselves—because they mask layers of hidden knowledge that would be necessary for the technique to be effectively used. Techniques per se, in other words, are examples of explicit knowledge and are only the tip of the iceberg. It is much harder, and more essential, to get at the first principles: the feel and understanding that comes with tacit knowledge. It is those first principles that constitute the value of the technique, not the mere use of the technique for its own sake.

Learning in context also makes it clear why (and how) modeling and mentoring are crucial. Mentors who evidence moral purpose, display emotional intelligence, and foster caring relationships and norms of reciprocity for knowledge sharing, show the way. When leaders model and promote all of these values and practices in the organization, they improve the performance of the organization while simultaneously developing new leadership all the time. In this sense, organizational performance and leadership development are *one and the same.*

If you want to develop leadership, you should focus on reciprocity, the mutual obligation and value of sharing knowledge among organizational members. The key to developing leadership is to develop knowledge and share it; if it is not mutually shared, it won't be adequately developed in the first place and will not be available to the organization in any case. For the individual, the explicit value to be internalized is the responsibility for sharing what you know. For the organization (or for leadership, if you like), the obligation is to remove barriers to sharing, create mechanisms for sharing, and reward those who do share. Leadership creates the conditions for individual and organizational development to merge.

Learning in context is based on the premise that "what is gained as a group must be shared as a group" (Pascale, Millemann, & Gioja, 2000, p. 264). Von Krogh, Ichijo, and Nonaka (2000) make a similar point:

> Allocate substantial time to think carefully through the types of knowledge you have in your business and where it resides. Is this critical knowledge for doing business kept in instructions, procedures, documents, and databases? Or is it tightly

connected to the skills of individual professionals, deeply rooted in their years of experience? If the answer is yes to the second question, do these professionals operate according to care-based values, allowing younger team members to acquire their skills through mentoring processes? If yes to this question, do you recognize the role of these people in the organization, and have you given them incentives to keep contributing to the company's overall knowledge [p. 263]?

Leaders, then, look for many opportunities to "cause" and reward leadership at all levels of the organization. When there is widespread learning in context, leadership for the future is a natural by-product.

Leadership for Many

There are two levels at which this book is about leadership for many: one obvious and one more fundamental. At the obvious level, the ideas in every chapter invite all of us to practice becoming better leaders, whether we are a rank-and-file employee, head of a committee, department head, manager, principal, or a high-ranking executive.

The other, more fundamental conclusion is that internal commitment ("energies internal to human beings that are activated because getting the job done is intrinsically rewarding" [Argyris, 2000, p. 40]) cannot be activated from the top. It must be nurtured up close in the dailiness of organizational behavior, and for that to happen there must be many leaders around us. Large organizations can never achieve perfect internal commitment, but with good leadership at all levels they can generate a great deal of it, and this will feed on itself.

When Henry Mintzberg was asked in a recent interview what organizations have to do to ensure success over the next ten years, he responded: "They've got to build a strong core of people who really care about the place and who have ideas. Those ideas have to flow freely and easily through the organization. It's not a question of riding in with a great new chief executive on a great white horse. Because as soon as that person rides out, the whole thing collapses unless somebody can do it again. So it's a question of building strong institutions, not creating heroic leaders. Heroic leaders get in the way of strong institutions" (quoted in Bernhut, 2000, p. 23).

Strong institutions have many leaders at all levels. Those in a position to be leaders of leaders, such as the CEO, know that they do not run the place. They know that they are cultivating leadership in others; they realize that they are doing more than planning for their own succession—that if they "lead right," the organization will outgrow them. Thus, the ultimate leadership contribution is to develop leaders in the organization who can move the organization even further after you have left (see Lewin & Regine, 2000, p. 220).

A Time to Disturb

As we are "careening into the future" (Homer-Dixon, 2000b) is the very time we need leadership the most. Yet leadership in all institutions is in short supply and worsening. "Policy Focus Converges on Leadership" (2000), the cover article of the January 12 issue of *Education Week,* begins, "After years of work on structural changes—standards and testing and ways of holding students and schools accountable—the education policy world has turned its attention to the people charged with making the system work. Nowhere is the focus on the human element more prevalent than in the recent recognition of the importance of strong and effective leadership" (p. 1).

The subtitle of the article states, "Principals Wanted: Apply Just About Anywhere." The same could be said about the superintendency and about leaders in all institutions. Leadership appropriate for the times is a scarce commodity.

Leadership and *knowledge society* are the twin buzzwords in the new millennium. In the corporate world, leadership development as a field has become a billion-dollar business in a few short years (Conger & Benjamin, 1999, p. xi). In education, leadership academies abound, the most prominent example being the new National College for School Leadership in England, with a new state-of-the-art building at the University of Nottingham, which is also the site of the University's Computer Science Department, Business School, and School of Education. Many philanthropic organizations, including the Wallace-Reader's Digest Funds and the Bill and Melinda Gates Foundation, have made school leadership a top priority.

With all the attention focused on strong leaders, visions, standards, and the like, it would be easy to get this wrong. We can't solve the problem of producing better leaders for a culture of change by attempting to produce greater numbers of individual leaders with the desired traits. Elmore (2000, p. 25) rightly observes that by using such a strategy, the proportion of leaders "seldom grows larger than but one quarter to one third of the total population of classrooms, schools, or system."

Glenn and Gordon state, "Today many believe it is possible to shape the future, rather than simply prepare for a future which is a linear extrapolation of the present or a product of chance or fate. [Yet the] complexity, number, and frequency of choices seem to grow beyond the ability to know and decide. Skills development in concept formulation and communications seems to be decreasing relative to the requirements of an increasingly complicated world" (1997, p. 29).

Homer-Dixon (2000a, p. 211) further reports, "Yaneer Bar-Yam, the American complexity theorist, . . . argues that the level of complexity of modern human society has recently overtaken the complexity of any one person belonging to it. . . . [S]o as modern human society becomes more complex than we are individually, it begins to exceed our adaptive ability. In effect, we have too short a repertoire of responses to adjust effectively to our changing circumstances."

When responding to changing circumstances becomes this difficult, we need leaders who can combine the five core capacities discussed in this book. In a culture of complexity, the chief role of leadership is to mobilize the *collective capacity* to challenge difficult circumstances. Our only hope is that many individuals working in concert can become as complex as the society they live in.

One of the main conclusions I have drawn is that the requirements of knowledge societies bring education and business leadership closer than they have ever been before. Corporations need souls and schools need minds (and vice versa) if the knowledge society is to survive—sustainability demands it. New mutual respect and partnerships between the corporate and education worlds are needed, especially concerning leadership development—provided those partnerships are guided by the forces discussed in Chapters Two through Six.

These five themes, I have argued, contain the right dynamics and the checks and balances for simultaneously letting go and reining in. When leaders act in the ways recommended, they will disturb the future "in a manner that approximates the desired outcomes," to use Pascale et al.'s felicitous phrase (2000). Such leaders will also create leadership at all levels of the organization in a way that cannot quite be controlled but that will have built-in safeguards because of the very dynamics involved.

What is needed for sustainable performance, then, is leadership at many levels of the organization. Pervasive leadership has a greater likelihood of occurring if leaders work on mastering the five core capacities: moral purpose, understanding of the change process, building relationships, knowledge building, and coherence making. Achieving such mastery is less a matter of taking leadership training and more a case of slow knowing and learning in context with others at all levels of the organization.

Ultimately, your leadership in a culture of change will be judged as effective or ineffective not by who you are as a leader but by *what leadership you produce in others*. Tortoises, start your engines!

References

Argyris, C. (2000). *Flawed advice and the management trap*. New York: Oxford University Press.

Barber, M. (2000). *High expectations and standards*. Unpublished manuscript, Department for Education and Employment, London.

Beer, M., Eisenstat, R., & Spector, B. (1990). *The critical path to corporate renewal*. Boston, MA: Harvard Business School Press.

Bernhut, S. (2000, September-October). Henry Mintzberg in conversation. *Ivey Business Journal*, pp. 19–23.

Bernstein, P. (1996). *Against the gods*. New York: Wiley.

Bishop, B. (2000). *The strategic enterprise*. Toronto: Stoddart.

Block, P. (1987). *The empowered manager: Positive political skills at work*. San Francisco: Jossey-Bass.

Bolman, L., & Deal, T. (2000). *Escape from cluelessness*. New York: AMACOM.

Brown, J. S., & Duguid, P. (2000). *The social life of information*. Boston: Harvard Business School Press.

Bryk, A., Sebring, P., Kerbow, D., Rollow, S., & Easton, J. (1998). *Charting Chicago school reform.* Boulder, CO: Westview Press.

Charisma and loud shouting. (2000, November 10). *Times Education Supplement,* p. 28.

Claxton, G. (1997). *Hare brained and tortoise mind.* London: Fourth Estate.

Conger, J. A., & Benjamin, B. (1999). *Building leaders: How successful companies develop the next generation.* San Francisco: Jossey-Bass.

Darrah, C. (1993). Workplace training, workplace learning: A case study. *Human Organization, 54*(1), 31–41.

De Gues, A. (1997). *The living company.* Boston: Harvard Business School Press.

Dixon, N. (2000). *Common knowledge.* Boston: Harvard Business School Press.

Earl, L., Fullan, M., Leithwood, K., Watson, N., with Jantzi, D., Levin, B., & Torrance, N. (2000). Watching & learning: OISE/UT evaluation of the implementation of the National Literacy and Numeracy Strategies. London: Report commissioned by the Department for Education and Employment.

Elmore, R. F. (2000). *Building a new structure for school leadership.* Washington, D.C.: Albert Shanker Institute.

Elmore, R. F., & Burney, D. (1999). Investing in teacher learning: Staff development and instructional improvement. In L. Darling-Hammond & G. Sykes (Eds.), *Teaching as the learning profession: Handbook of policy and practice* (pp. 236–291). San Francisco: Jossey-Bass.

Fink, E., & Resnick, L. (1999). *Developing principals as instructional leaders.* Paper prepared for the High Performance Learning Communities Project, Learning Research and Development Center, University of Pittsburg.

Fullan, M. (1993). *Change forces: Probing the depths of educational reform.* London: Falmer Press.

Fullan, M. (1999). *Change forces: The sequel.* Bristol, PA: Falmer Press.

Fullan, M. (2001). *The new meaning of educational change* (3rd ed.). New York: Teachers College Press.

Fullan, M. (forthcoming). *Change forces with a vengeance.* London: Falmer Press.

Fullan, M., & Hargreaves, A. (1992). *What's worth fighting for? Working together for your school.* Toronto, Ontario: Elementary Teachers Federation of Ontario; New York: Teachers College Press.

Fullan, M., Alvarado, A., Bridges, R., & Green, N. (2000). *Review of administrative organization: Guilford County.* Toronto: Ontario Institute for Studies in Education.

Garten, J. (2001). *The mind of the CEO.* New York: Basic Books.

Garvin, D. (2000). *Learning in action.* Boston: Harvard Business School Press.

Gaynor, A. (1977). A study of change in educational organizations. In L. Cunningham (Ed.), *Educational administration* (pp. 28–40). Berkeley, CA: McCutcham.

Gleick, J. (1999). *Faster.* New York: Pantheon Books.

Glenn, J., & Gordon, T. (Ed.). (1997). *State of the future: Implications for action today.* Washington, D.C.: American Council for the United Nations University.

Goleman, D. (1995). *Emotional intelligence.* New York: Bantam Books.

Goleman, D. (1998). *Working with emotional intelligence.* New York: Bantam Books.

Goleman, D. (2000, March-April). Leadership that gets results. *Harvard Business Review,* pp. 78–90.

Goffee, R., & Jones, G. (2000, September-October). Why should anyone be led by you? *Harvard Business Review,* pp. 63–70.

Hamel, G. (2000). *Leading the revolution.* Boston: Harvard Business School Press.

Hatch, T. (2000). *What happens when multiple improvement initiatives collide.* Menlo Park, CA: Carnegie Foundation for the Advancement of Teaching.

Heifetz, R. (1994). *Leadership without easy answers.* Cambridge, MA: Harvard University Press.

Hess, F. M. (1999). *Spinning wheels: The politics of urban school reform.* Washington, D.C.: Brookings Institution.

Homer-Dixon, T. (2000a). *The ingenuity gap.* Toronto: Knopf.

Homer-Dixon, T. (2000b, November 24). *Leadership captive. Toronto Globe and Mail,* p. A15.

Johnson, S. M. (1996). *Leading to change: The challenge of the new superintendency.* San Francisco: Jossey-Bass.

Knowledge officer aims to spread the word. (2000, October 30). *Toronto Globe and Mail,* p. M1.

Kotter, J. (1996). *Leading change.* Boston: Harvard Business School Press.

Kouzes, J. M., & Posner, B. Z. (1998). *Encouraging the heart: A leader's guide to rewarding and recognizing others.* San Francisco: Jossey-Bass.

Leadership Academy at University of San Diego, The. (2000). *San Diego: Joint initiative of the San Diego School District and the University of San Diego.*

Lewin, R., & Regine, B. (2000). *The soul at work.* New York: Simon & Schuster.

Lortie, D. (1975). School teacher: A sociological study. Chicago: University of Chicago Press.

Martin, J. B. (1968). *Campaign journal.* John Barlow Martin papers. Washington, DC: Library of Congress.

Maurer, R. (1996). *Beyond the wall of resistance.* Austin, TX: Bard Books.

McLaughlin, M., & Talbert, J. (2001). *Professional Communities and the Work of High-School Teaching.* Chicago: University of Chicago Press.

Micklethwait, J., & Wooldridge, A. (1996). *The witch doctors: Making sense of management gurus.* New York: Random House.

Mintzberg, H., Ahlstrand, B., & Lampel, J. (1998). *Strategy safari: A guided tour through the wilds of strategic management.* New York: Free Press.

Newmann, F., King, B., & Youngs, P. (2000, April). *Professional development that addresses school capacity.* Paper presented at the annual meeting of the American Educational Research Association. New Orleans.

Nonaka, I., & Takeuchi, H. (1995). *The knowledge-creating company.* Oxford: Oxford University Press.

Palmer, P. (1998). *The courage to teach.* San Francisco: Jossey-Bass.

Pascale, R., Millemann, M., & Gioja, L. (2000). *Surfing the edge of chaos.* New York: Crown Business Publishing.

Peters, T., & Waterman, R. (1982). *In search of excellence.* New York: HarperCollins.

Policy focus converges on leadership. (2000, January 12). *Education Week,* (16), pp. 1, 17.

Polyani, M. (1983). *The tacit dimension.* Gloucester, MA: Peter Smith.

Ridley, M. (1996). *The origins of virtue.* Harmondsworth, England: Penguin Books.

Senge, P., Cambron-McCabe, N., Lucas, T., Smith, B., Dutton, J., & Kleiner, A. (2000). *Schools that learn.* New York: Doubleday.

Sergiovanni, T. J. (1999). *The lifeworld of leadership: Creating culture, community, and personal meaning in our schools.* San Francisco: Jossey-Bass.

Sober, E., & Wilson, D. (1998). *Unto others: The evolution and psychology of unselfish behavior.* Cambridge, MA: Harvard University Press.

Stacey, R. (2000). *Strategic management and organizational dynamics* (3rd ed.). London: Prentice Hall.

Stanford University. (2000a). *San Diego principal survey.* Palo Alto: Center for the Study of Teaching and Policy, Stanford University.

Stanford University. (2000b). *The San Diego City Schools Reform Initiative: Views from the inside.* Palo Alto: Center for the Study of Teaching and Policy, Stanford University.

Stein, S., & Book, H. (2000). *The EQ edge.* Toronto: Stoddart.

Storr, A. (1997). *Feet of clay: A study of gurus.* London: HarperCollins.

Thomas, E. (2000). *Robert Kennedy: His life.* New York: Simon & Schuster.

Von Krogh, G., Ichijo, K., & Nonaka, I. (2000). *Enabling knowledge creation: How to unlock the mystery of tacit knowledge and release the power of innovation.* Oxford: Oxford University Press.

About the Author

Michael Fullan is the former Dean of the Ontario Institute for Studies in Education of the University of Toronto. Recognized as an international authority on educational reform, Michael is engaged in training, consulting, and evaluating change projects around the world. His ideas for managing change are used in many countries, and his books have been published in many languages.

Michael Fullan led the evaluation team which conducted the four-year assessment of the National Literacy and Numeracy Strategy in England from 1998–2003. In April 2004 he was appointed Special Advisor to the Premier and Minister of Education in Ontario. His widely acclaimed books include: *Leading in a Culture of Change, What's Worth Fighting For, Change Forces, The New Meaning of Educational Change, Third Edition, The Moral Imperative of School Leadership, Leadership and Sustainability: Systems Thinkers in Action.*

Index

Discussion Questions

1. What core leadership values and practices does Fullan consider as required at all levels of an organization? How can those values and practices be acquired and applied by any leader?

2. How, according to Fullan, can leaders in any organization significantly improve their knowledge and performance? How can they bring about systematic, permanent, and positive change?

3. What are the five core competencies articulated by Fullan, how does he see them as providing for coherence within organizations, and how might you apply those competencies within the organizations or practices in which you are active? How does Fullan present, throughout the book, each of the five core competencies of effective leadership? How does he relate each to the others?

4. How can leaders go about fostering leadership in others, "thereby making themselves dispensable in the long run" (p. x)? Why might any leader want to make herself or himself indispensable? "Ultimately," Fullan writes in his closing paragraph, "your leadership in a culture of change will be judged as effective or ineffective not by who you are as a leader but by *what leadership you produce in others*" (p. 137). How do Fullan's five core competencies of effective leadership, along with other key principles he identifies, contribute to producing leadership in others?

5.   In what ways, according to Fullan, are businesses and schools similar "in the knowledge society. . .at the most basic level" (p. xi)? What similar challenges do business and education leaders face? In what ways and to what degree do Fullan's "five components of leadership represent independent but mutual reinforcing forces for positive change" (p. 3)?

6.   How might understanding the process of change and a "respect for the complexities of the change process . . . . unearth deeper moral purpose" (p. 5)? What are the "six guidelines that provide leaders with concrete and novel ways of thinking about the process of change," (p. 5) and how do these guidelines function?

7.   Fullan presents case studies of "more good things happening" and "fewer bad things happening" as the outcomes of effective leadership and commitment. Using the "Framework of Leadership" in Figure 1.1 (p. 4) and one of Fullan's case studies as a model, prepare a case study of your own showing how this framework of leadership resulted in more good things and fewer bad things, or how its breakdown resulted in fewer good things and more bad things.

8.   Fullan writes that "leaders in all organizations, whether they know it or not, contribute for better or for worse to moral purpose in their own organizations and society as a whole" (p. 15). Discuss or prepare reports on the ways in which various leaders, historical or contemporary, illustrate that statement.

9.   What signs does Fullan identify "that moral purpose is on the ascendancy in schools and businesses" (p. 27)? What additional signs can you identify? On the other hand, what instances can you identify in which moral purpose was—or is—absent from the operations of educational and business organizations?

10. How might Fullan's six guidelines to "Understanding the Change Process" (p. 34) result in more effective leadership?

What examples does he give of each of these guidelines in practice? How would you apply these guidelines to your organization?

11. What does Fullan mean by "reculturing," and why is it so important in his view of effective leadership and organizational growth and success?

12. What is complexity science, and why must effective leaders "cultivate their knowledge, understanding, and skills" of complexity science (p. 45)? How do self-organizing and strange attractors, two of the concepts in complexity science, relate to coherence making? How do they inform the performance of successful leaders?

13. Fullan writes that R. Lewin and B. Regine, in *The Soul at Work,* "make the case that there is a new style of leadership in successful companies—one that focuses on people and relationships as essential to getting sustained results" (p. 53). What evidence does Fullan provide to support the essential importance of relationships in successful organizations? What examples can you identify of organizations in which a focus on relationships contributed to sustained success and of organizations where the absence of such a focus resulted in lackluster performance or failure?

14. On pages 54–55, Fullan cites the "seven essentials to developing relationships" identified by J. M. Kouzes and B. Z. Posner in *Encouraging the Heart: A Leader's Guide to Rewarding and Recognizing Others.* How do you think each of those seven essentials could be—or should be—applied in either a business or school? What examples of each have you observed or experienced?

15. Fullan writes that "leaders in a culture of change require a quality that all long-term effective leaders have—the capacity to resist a focus on short-term gains at the expense of deeper reform where gains are steady but not necessarily dramatic. Unlike businesses that go for immediate profit,

schools should resist going for an immediate boost in test scores" (p. 63). In a culture that still seems to focus on short-term business profits and immediate test-score achievement, how might the changes that Fullan calls for be put into effect? What might you do to contribute to effective leadership in our culture of change?

16. What does Fullan mean by the term "emotional intelligence"? How would you support or refute his statement that "the most effective leaders are not the smartest in an IQ sense but are those who combine intellectual brilliance with emotional intelligence"? What examples does he provide in support of his statement? How can emotional intelligence be learned and improved?

17. "Effective leaders," writes Fullan, "understand the value and role of knowledge creation, they make it a priority and set about establishing and reinforcing habits of knowledge exchange among organizational members" (p. 87). How would you go about establishing and reinforcing such habits? What mechanisms and procedures would you establish to facilitate effective habits of knowledge exchange?

18. What are the three major "hidden" features of the process of coherence making, and how do they contribute to greater overall coherence?

19. In his final chapter Fullan identifies "three powerful lessons about leadership that have implications for developing more of it" (p. 121). What are those lessons? How are they interrelated? What role does each have in the development and application of effective leadership?

20. What can you do personally to become more effective in "leading in a culture of change"? Identify two or three actions you could take in this direction.

21. This discussion guide was prepared by Hal Hager, of Hal Hager & Associates, Somerville, New Jersey.